FBI Code Name:

SPYTRAP

Washington Seduction

A SPECIAL AGENT DEL DICKERSON NOVEL

Jim Healy

Published by Jimbay Books

© 2017 Jim Healy

All rights reserved. No portion of this book may be reproduced, stored in a retrieval system, or transmitted in any form or by any means-electronic, mechanical, photo-copy, recording, scanning or other–except for brief quotations in critical reviews or articles, without the prior permission of the author.

Book Cover Design by Terry-Cox Joseph

ISBN-13: 978-0-9904952-77

Disclaimer: **FBI Code Name: SPYTRAP,** *Washington Seduction***,** is a work of fiction, based on a wide variety of characters encountered during the author's FBI career. Any resemblance to actual persons, living or deceased, is coincidental and unintentional, and merely reflects the author's imagination.

DEDICATION

This book is dedicated to unsung FBI heroes—undercover and surveillance agents who often labor in obscurity to safeguard the American public while engaged day and night in perilous assignments. Their selfless, unheralded efforts exemplify the proud traditions embodied in the FBI motto, *Fidelity, Bravery, Integrity.*

You, and your associates, know who you are. Thanks for your honorable service.

Jim Healy, Author

Chapter One

WASHINGTON, D.C.

They will never check there, the full-figured brunet told herself as she slid the CD into the lined pouch attached to the front of her frilly black panties.

Exiting a stall in the otherwise empty embassy lounge, she studied her reflection in the full-length mirror, satisfied with the concealment.

Fifteen minutes later, she breezed through the security magnetometer and paused while the chatty guard examined the purse she had placed on the conveyor belt. "Looks like you're going to a party, Nadia. That's a pretty dress."

"Thanks, Norman. Embassy reception. Command appearance."

"Have a good time," the uniformed guard said, handing her the purse. "You'll knock them dead."

"You always say the nicest things," the woman replied, shooting Norman a dazzling smile that illuminated her intriguing features.

Five minutes later, she slid into the back seat of a cab that had abruptly swerved to the curb. "Hello, Viktor," she greeted the driver. "Perfect timing."

"Always good to see you," the driver said as he moved into heavy Massachusetts Avenue traffic. "Everything go well?"

"Smoothly," she said, fumbling under her flowing skirt and reaching down. "It's under the floor mat."

"Nice work. Any suspicion?"

"No, it's a workable system. A little uncomfortable at times."

The driver glanced back in his rear-view mirror at his attractive passenger. "All warmed up for me? Gives me a feeling of closeness."

"Don't get any ideas, Viktor. Private property."

The woman carefully rearranged her undergarments before adding, "We all have a job to do, Viktor. Let me out near the entrance of the Chinese Embassy. And keep your pants on."

"Suka," (Bitch) the cabbie muttered.

"Here's your fare," the woman said, passing a twenty-dollar bill over the seat back. "Hold it high, in case someone is watching."

"Cheapskate," Viktor grunted as he grabbed the bill.

Not cheap, Nadia thought with a sense of sadness as she exited the cab. Forcing a bright smile, she approached the glittering, flag-adorned diplomatic establishment. *Will I ever be free?*

* * *

Special Agent Joe Moretti addressed his partner in the concealed FBI observation post overlooking the embassy entrance. "Get the number of the cab that dropped the well-dressed woman?"

"Yep," the colleague replied. "It's from a small taxi company in Arlington. Should be easy to trace. And the driver looked vaguely familiar."

"I noticed the lady paid in cash. Did you note the denomination?"

Harry Swanson laughed. "No, my lens isn't that good, but she didn't get any change. Nice looking gal, from my angle. Hope our outside troops can identify her."

"Me too," Moretti said, "but it may take some time with the work load and manpower shortage."

Swanson kept his camera-equipped high-power binoculars focused on his target. "I understand they're bringing in more agents from the field, including a Korean-speaking guy from California to work on the South Korean Embassy probe. He's supposed to be quite a character, with fabulous luck."

"That we need," Moretti concurred, taking another sip of keep-awake lukewarm lookout coffee.

TYSONS CORNER, VA

"Good Lord, say it isn't true!" Andy Dutton exclaimed with a pained expression. The Assistant Special Agent in Charge of the Northern Virginia satellite office of the metropolitan Washington FBI Division had just been informed of the identity of the Special Agent coming to assist in a sensitive investigation.

Kevin Ryan, the agent supervising the case raised his eyebrows. "A problem, boss? You don't look so good."

Dutton sighed. "A giant problem. That guy has gotten into more weird situations in his brief Bureau career than most agents experience in a lifetime. He was here on the SHARKS special, before you arrived, and damned near caused us all to have heart attacks. He's a supervisory nightmare. But," Dutton added in a grudging tone, "he does enjoy fantastic luck."

"We could use some luck," Ryan replied. "We're stuck in neutral on the investigation of the intelligence leak at the South Korean Embassy. Someone is stealing high-level data damaging to both of our countries. I felt the need for a Korean- speaking agent, so I called Personnel at headquarters. My contact there told me this was my lucky day—said he had just the guy for us. He recently graduated from the Language School in Monterey. Finished near the top of his class. The Personnel man did mention that the guy is smart, but sort of unorthodox—attracts trouble like a bear to honey, but always lands on his feet. He also said that the guy has a strong appeal to women."

"That's him," Dutton said. "Del Dickerson. Really think he could help?"

"Yeah, we need someone to stir things up."

"Oh, I'm certain he'll do that. Are you ready to jeopardize your future? I can retire any time."

Ryan nodded. "I was a Navy SEAL before joining the Bureau. One of our mottos is *'The Only Easy Day Was Yesterday.'*"

"Okay, Kevin. Tell headquarters to send him on. I believe he's currently assigned to San Francisco. By the way, his nickname is 'Delbert the Disaster.'"

SAN FRANCISCO

Special Agent Del Dickerson had just returned from a surveillance when he was summoned to his supervisor's office in the FBI Field Office on Golden Gate Avenue. Ralph Monroe waved him onto a chair. "Are your cases up to date?"

Del mentally reviewed his case load. "Believe so, Ralph. Why?"

"Keeping up with your Korean?"

"Yeah, but haven't had much use for it so far."

"Would you like to put your language skills to work?"

"Definitely. Don't want to get rusty after all that effort."

"Well, you will have your chance. Ready to travel?"

"Sure, that's part of the job, isn't it? Why all the questions?"

"We just heard from Washington. They need your services back there. They're sending more details. They want you to report to the Tysons Corner R.A."

Del smiled. "Hey, I worked there in the SHARKS Special. Had a lot of fun."

"We'll miss you here," Monroe said with a grin. "You seem to have fun wherever you go. We haven't had as much fun since you diverted that gay rights parade through the Masonic Temple last month."

"Yeah, that was a blast. It kept the marchers from disrupting the mayor's rally on Nob Hill."

"Right, for which he was very grateful," Monroe recalled. "Your reputation for unusual good luck lives on."

"It's not always good, Ralph. Remember the fugitive roundup party we hosted at the Moscone Center when we arrested a half dozen of the P.D.'s snitches?"

"Oh, do I remember! Took a lot of charm school snake oil to calm the Police Chief down. It did bag twenty-five fugitives, though. Where did you get that idea?"

"Nothing original. Heard of other offices using the technique. We just localized it. Spread the word through the hood that there would be a big party with free booze and eats, and lots of chicks and a hot band and waited for the guests to arrive. Staffed the scene with our undercover folks. Once the party started we invited those we had warrants for to step into an adjoining room one by one for some special 'smoke.' Then we slapped on the cuffs and hustled them out the back way while the party went on. We ran out of cuffs before we had to shut it down. Twenty-five fugitives—not a bad night's work—and no travel time."

"Don't forget the six P.D. informants."

"Yeah, you never know what the net will catch when you dip it into the water."

"Well, I hope your luck holds where you're headed. I understand it involves big fish."

"We hope and pray," Del said solemnly. "Now I need to tell Anna."

* * *

Del and his fiancée, Anna Chen, were seated at a window table at their favorite Fisherman's Wharf restaurant, feasting on one of SCOMAS' famed Crab Louis dishes.

"We always seem to be parting," the raven-haired Amerasian beauty said with a tone of sadness.

"Yes," her sandy-haired partner agreed. "But it should only be for a brief period. If we're lucky."

Anna smiled. "Isn't that your middle name?"

"Sometimes, but haven't we both been lucky and blessed? I'm hoping that our good fortune continues."

"Always the optimist—one of your special qualities," she said, reaching out to pat his hand. "Guess this puts our wedding plans on hold for a while."

"It won't be for long, honey. With any luck, I'll be back before you know it."

"Ah, that magic word," Anna said, taking a sip of her Louis Martini chardonnay and leaning back in her chair at the same time a departing patron jostled a passing waiter carrying a heavy array of food. Forced against the back of Anna's chair, the waiter watched with dismay as a plate of fried calamari slid off his tray and landed in the center of their table. A cup of marinara sauce flew into the air.

Del ducked as a stream of red sauce sailed past his ear and splattered against the window.

Anna wasn't as fortunate, feeling a chunky glob strike her right cheek. Stunned but composed as she delicately used her napkin to remove the spot, she managed a grin. "Not much debate who is the lucky one, is there?"

* * *

Two morning's later, Del's office buddy, Special Agent Tommy Kwan, delivered his partner to the American Airlines curbside check-in stand at San Francisco International Airport. Anna, dressed for work at the Pier 39 Emporium in a Chinese-accented golden sheath, clung possessively to Del's hand, basking in the pleasant recollection of their previous night's passionate farewell. "Now, behave yourself back there," she said as they concluded a parting kiss.

"Scout's honor," Del proclaimed, raising his right hand in a three-finger salute.

Tommy Kwan felt his own fingers unconsciously cross.

Chapter Two

TYSONS CORNER

"Hello again, Mr. Dutton," Del greeted, extending his hand. "Good to see you. Bet you didn't expect me back so soon?"

The Assistant Special Agent in Charge suppressed his initial thought and returned a firm handshake. "Welcome back, Del. The place hasn't been the same since you went West. Looks like it agrees with you."

"Love it out there, sir. Can't wait to get back."

Dutton stifled an agreeing thought. "Help us solve our problem here and make it happen."

"I'll do my best, boss. With any luck we'll make it fast."

Let us pray, Dutton reflected. "Meet Kevin Ryan. He has the ticket, and will explain the situation."

A dark-haired man in his mid-thirties rose from his chair and shook hands. "Pleased to meet you," the supervising agent said in a clipped New England voice.

"Massachusetts?" Del asked.

"Boston College," Ryan replied with a smile. "You're good at dialects."

"Language School overload perhaps," Del responded. "Actually, I lived with a lot of Micks in college."

"Yale, I understand."

"Please don't hold that against me. I've become Americanized in the Bureau."

Ryan laughed. "Looks like we can work together."

Dutton broke in. "If you two are finished bonding, let's get down to business. You'll have plenty of time later to discuss fraternities and bloodlines."

Ryan nodded and produced a thick packet that he opened on the conference table. "Pull up a chair. Here's what we have: Someone penetrated the intelligence operations of the South Korean Embassy, and we've been getting feedback from other sources of bits of data we've shared with them. Our CI agents have been working around the clock with the ROK security folks but can't put a finger on the leak. It has to be on a high level, and they've narrowed down possibilities but so far no luck." He paused for a sip of water, and picked up another document.

"With the increasing North Korean nuclear weapons program, some important people are getting quite nervous. The Korean-speaking agent who has been working the case is going on maternity leave, so we asked the Bureau for help. They sent you."

Del grinned. "Well, you don't have to worry about me getting pregnant. What do you want me to do?"

"Review the case files and get involved in Korean social activities. There's a large Korean community in Northern Virginia, and a lot of martial arts facilities they frequent. One we are particularly interested in is located in Annandale. They teach Tae Kwon Do. Ever hear of it?"

"Yes, in fact. We studied Korean culture at the Language School. It means roughly, the way of foot and fist. Very athletic. You can work your way up to a prized black belt."

"Well, we want you to join the Annandale studio, under an assumed name, and start making friends. Here's some business cards. You'll recognize the name."

Del studied the cards and laughed. "Del Dixon. That's the alias I used in the SHARKS case." He immediately thought of Anna, and how they met.

"We checked the files," Ryan said. "Lots of interesting personal data about you there. Anyway, you sell insurance for a national company that will back up your employment if anyone inquires. The significance of the Annandale location is that one of the leak possibilities, a translator at the South Korean Embassy, frequents that studio. Get to know her. Her name is Nadia Rostov. Here's her picture."

"Nice looking," Del said. "Name sounds Russian."

"It is, and you wonder why she's working at the South Korean Embassy?"

"Yeah."

"Simple. She's reportedly a whiz at languages—Russian, German, English, Chinese and Korean."

"I met a few brilliant linguists like that at the Language School. Wasn't being Russian, no pun intended, a security red flag?"

"No question, but they say she was extensively vetted. Her family fled to the U.S. to escape Commie persecution. She is supposedly a devout Orthodox Christian. And, she is heavily into physical fitness. So, one of your first jobs is to eliminate or nail her as a suspect. Not a bad assignment, I'd say. Just be aware of the honey pots."

"I've heard of them," Del said. "Something to be avoided."

Ryan nodded emphatically. "Absolutely. Nothing but trouble. Here's a brief on their history, and recent Bureau experiences. It includes details of our Anna Chapman investigation that resulted in her arrest with nine others in New York in 2010. She was a star Russian spy, and homeland heroine for seducing her targets. Russia isn't the only country to utilize female spies, of course. It's as old as history. Remember Mata Hari? There's a long history of using women to gather intelligence. The Russians even have a special training school in the 'art'. After former KGB General Oleg Kalugin defected to the U.S., he was asked why they used so many women in their spy work. He reportedly answered, 'in America, in the West, occasionally you ask your men to stand up for their country. There's little difference. In Russia, we just ask our young women to lay down.'"

ASAC Dutton added his admonition. "The message is clear, Del. Be alert all the time, and don't fall into a honey trap."

Del picked up the printed material and nodded solemnly. "You can count on me."

Dutton thought of past experiences with his unpredictable young charge and felt his pulse quicken. *That's what I'm afraid of.*

ANNANDALE, VA

The smiling manager was impressed with the way the tall Caucasian spoke his native language. "We are most pleased that you have selected our humble studio, Mr. Dixon."

"You enjoy a good reputation, Mr. Kim. I just started my study of the art on the west coast, and wish to pursue my interest."

"Well, you've come to the right place. Our clientele includes all ages, and is co-ed. And, we have a skilled Master dedicated to satisfying our followers. Let me show you our facilities."

Del followed the lithe instructor through the studio, noting mostly energetic youngsters bouncing and kicking all over the padded mats. "Lots of children," Del commented.

"Oh, it's different at night. Many adults."

"Good, I wouldn't like to be thrown around by a little kid."

"No problem, Mr. Dixon. I can assure you a full-size opponent to grapple with. Do you have a dubok?"

"A what?"

"A Tae Kwon Do uniform—sparring gear."

"Oh, that. I forgot its name, but I left everything out west."

"No problem. I can loan you some gear until you get your own. When do you want to get started?"

"The sooner the better," Del asserted. "I'll be back tomorrow evening."

"Splendid," the manager said, tightly grasping Del's cash deposit.

BURKE LAKE PARK, FAIRFAX, VA

Nadia Rostov jogged away from a fitness path and slid onto a bench on the fringe of a remote unused amphitheater, resting her Adidas-clad feet on an adjoining bench. She was joined two minutes later by a husky black-haired man in a blue running suit. "Nice day," the man greeted. "You are looking well."

"Thank you. Here's my report on the Chinese Embassy reception," she said, handing him a thin envelope.

"Good news?"

"Perhaps. A staffer from the French Embassy with too much to drink confided to me that the Americans have assigned an agent with unique talents to find the leak at my embassy. It's getting too close."

The man smiled. "Was the confidence perhaps revealed on a pillow?"

Natalie responded with a cold stare, reminded of the encounter with the amorous diplomat in his steamy hotel suite. "Mudak." (Asshole) she said.

"You're good at what you do, Nadia," the man replied in a placating tone. "We respect that."

"I'm glad to hear that. What I do isn't easy. I'm also getting nervous about the 'equipment' we're using, Alexei. A thorough body search will disclose it."

"You can put your pretty mind to rest, my dear. We have anticipated that possibility. You now have a new device that should prove virtually impossible to detect." He handed her a lipstick-sized tube, and smiled. "You know where it fits. Thank our Chinese comrades for the design."

Natalie retorted, "It would fit in a man too, wouldn't it?"

The man released a hearty laugh. "I've always enjoyed your spirit, Nadia. But you're the one on the inside. We need a few more essential details of their plans."

"And then I am finished?"

The man stroked his thick mustache. "There may be other needs for your 'services.'"

She sighed. "How much is expected in serving their country?"

"Remember what your grandparents have sacrificed."

Nadia stood. "I never forget."

"You will be well rewarded. Another deposit was made today in your bank account. Time to go. We meet next time by the carousel, near the waiting line. One hour earlier."

"Good, that makes it easier to get to my Tae Kwon Do class on time."

His eyes roamed over her shapely form. "You stay in tempting condition, Nadia. Do you get to wrestle with men there?"

"We don't call it wrestling, Alexei, but there is some physical contact with others. It is considered an art."

"Like your other art?"

"Poshyolnahui," (Fuck you) she blurted, heading for the adjacent path where she almost collided with two young runners jogging in tandem.

* * *

"Did you get a good photo of them?" the jogger in a burgundy running suit asked his partner.

"Hope so," his gold-clad companion replied. "Nice looking woman. We know who he is. Now we need to find out who she is."

Chapter Three

BURKE LAKE PARK

"Damn, a flat tire," Special Agent Curtis Oswald exclaimed to his partner as they hurried to follow the woman in the snug white running suit who had just hopped into a silver Toyota.

"And there she goes," Special Agent Cynthia Chalmers sighed, watching their target's SUV fade from sight.

"Did you catch the plate number?" Oswald asked hopefully.

"No, but it looked like a Virginia license."

"Which is logical since we're in Virginia."

"Don't need to be sarcastic, Curt."

Oswald smirked. "Just observing. No need to be touchy."

"Okay, we blew the surveillance. I told Kevin we needed another unit."

"I agree. 'Manpower limitations' is becoming a lame excuse. They better give us some help soon if they expect good results."

"It's on the way, I hear."

"Promises, promises," the trim blonde in the gold workout gear replied. "Typical male-speak."

"Kevin works for a female supervisor, blondie."

"All right, it's a draw. Who's going to change the tire?"

"Guess it's a man's job," Oswald said.

"We're not helpless, Curt. Radio in what happened while I do the honors. I learned the trade while working in my dad's garage."

"Not just a pretty face, then?" Oswald said with a grin, watching his comely partner unlimber the jack.

ANNANDALE, VA

Del felt encouraged when he saw several adults enter the Tae Kwon Do studio. Unfortunately, none of them fit the description of Nadia Rostov.

Dressed in his borrowed dubok, he participated in limbering up exercises and watched various clients pairing up for sparring matches. When he decided his muscles were ready for further exertion, he made his way to the expansive mats and caught the attention of the studio Master.

"Good evening, Mr. Dixon. We're honored to have you join our humble spa."

"My pleasure, sir. I'm anxious to learn more of the art."

"We will do our best to accommodate your wishes. Mr. Kim will be pleased to spar with you," he said, signaling to the Manager.

After a few minutes of stumbling around the mat, Del paused for breath. "Your skills are way beyond mine, Mr. Kim."

"Only a matter of time, Mr. Dixon, but perhaps someone also new to the art might be a fairer match. Would you mind a female opponent?"

"No," Del was replying when he spotted a dark-haired woman entering the studio.

"Ah," Kim said, "we just might have our answer. Ms. Rostov is also a recent member of our studio. Let me introduce you."

Can't get much better than this, Del was thinking when the woman acknowledged the instructor's signal and joined them.

More attractive than her photo, Del concluded as introductions were made. He noticed her slight accent. Nadia and Del were the names exchanged as they began their first match following a formal bow.

She's good, Del realized as Nadia deftly thrust an impressive variety of jabs and kicks. His efforts were clumsy by comparison. After several minutes of exertion they paused.

"You are very skilled," he complimented.

Her smile was disarming. "Thank you. I see latent talents in you."

"I have a lot to learn. You are very diplomatic."

Her laugh was gentle. "Perhaps my surroundings. I work in a diplomatic establishment."

Del nodded. "I thought I detected an accent. Slavic?"

"You have a keen ear. Russian."

"An intriguing culture," Del replied.

"But that's not where I work," Nadia volunteered.

Del looked questioning.

"I'm employed at the South Korean Embassy as a translator."

"Joheun jeonyeok," Del said with a broad smile.

Her eyes brightened. "And a good evening to you. You sound fluent in Korean."

"I studied the fascinating language."

"What a delightful discovery," the woman said. "Shall we try another match?"

This is too easy, Del told himself, taking a position on the mat.

This guy is too convenient, Nadia's instincts concluded as she faced her opponent.

Moving around cautiously, Del made a conscious effort to repress knowledge of the personal weapons of defense learned at the FBI Academy and regularly practiced by Bureau agents, responding awkwardly to his opponent's skillful movements. He was impressed with her athletic agility while noting her piercing brown eyes and pleasing figure, only partly concealed by her exercise jacket.

Nadia demonstrated cool determination as she launched forceful kicks and punches, some alarmingly close to striking her target. While dodging one vigorous thrust, Del slipped and failed to evade the assault, shocked by a clenched fist soundly impacting his left eye. Stars sparkled as the action stopped with Nadia's exclamation, "Oh my Lord! I didn't mean to strike you. I'm so sorry!"

Del stood stunned as the manager rushed up to examine the injury. "We are mortified, Mr. Dixon. This rarely happens. We need to put a cold compress on it to restrain swelling. How does it feel?"

"Like being kicked by a horse," he responded with a grin, glancing at Nadia who looked devastated. "Excuse that phrase," he quickly added. "I know it was accidental, and probably my fault. But you do pack quite a wallop."

"Please forgive me," she said, regaining her poise with a pleading smile, "but you'll have a reminder of our introduction."

"I'm a marked man," Del joked.

Maybe more than you think, Nadia ruminated.

TYSONS CORNER

"What the hell happened?" FBI Supervisor Kevin Ryan asked with alarm the next morning as he stared at Del's swollen eye that displayed a rainbow of colors.

Del grinned. "I did what you told me to do. I met Nadia Rostov."

"She did that to you?"

"Yep. One punch. She's a tough lady."

"Okay, what's the story? The ASAC will want to know everything."

Del reported his experience in detail, concluding by mentioning his next scheduled Tae Kwon Do session.

Ryan scratched his head. "Think you can survive another bout with the lady?"

"Willing to try," Del said with a smile. "She's quite attractive."

"Remember what we warned about— honey pots."

"Never forget it. You can tell Mr. Dutton not to worry."

"Any hints she's on to you? Think she bought your Del Dixon insurance man story?"

"Believe so. I'll have a better idea with more exposure to her."

"That's what we're concerned about—exposure. Be careful."

"Roger, Kevin. I've been in tempting situations before."

"We know," Ryan replied, sensing an increasing heartbeat. "By the way," he said changing topics, "we identified the cabbie who dropped her at the Chinese Embassy the other night. Viktor Markov, a Russian emigre known to run errands for the SVR. That tightens the possibility that Nadia's the Korean Embassy leak. We have to play her delicately."

"You can count on me," Del reasserted.

GEORGETOWN, WASHINGTON, D.C.

She was seated at a small table at the rear of the small Wisconsin Avenue café. Dinner patrons had largely disappeared as Nadia lingered over her tea. Her late afternoon call to a telephone number committed to memory, requesting an emergency meeting, was answered by a curt "seven p.m." The recipient of her call was now approaching her table.

"This better be important," the man in a black leather jacket said as he slid onto a chair opposite hers.

"I wouldn't have called if it wasn't, Alexei. I believe they have put an operative on me. They're on to us."

"Don't panic," the cultural attaché at the Russian Embassy cautioned. "Tell me why you think that."

Nadia related her experience with Del. "He claims to be an insurance salesman."

"Derrmo. (Shit) You were so close to getting the last few details of the plans that are urgently needed. Do you think that's still possible?"

Nadia's expression was grim. "It'll be risky, but I believe so."

"You'll be well rewarded, you know," the man said. "See if you can confirm that he's a plant. When is your next contact with him?"

"Tomorrow night, if he shows up at the Tae Kwon Do studio after his accident."

"Accident?"

"I gave him a black eye."

Alexei Nikolay smiled. "That's not your usual style. Use you charms."

"We'll see," Nadia said, placing the envelope the man left on the table in her purse.

"Be careful," the man warned as he bid farewell.

* * *

As Nadia rose to leave, she paid little attention to the young couple at the bar who had arrived shortly after the Russian, and were now photographing each other and their surroundings with an I-phone.

Chapter Four

ANNANDALE, VA

"Good evening," Nadia greeted Del as both assembled with other Tae Kwon Do enthusiasts at the exercise studio. "Please again accept my apologies for the black eye."

"No need for that, Nadia. It was my clumsy footwork. And it's not really black," he said, pointing to the rainbow of colors surrounding the socket.

"I imagine you would welcome a less combative partner tonight," she said.

"Oh, no. I'd be honored to spar with you again. I'll just try to be a bit more nimble."

"You're a gracious gentleman, Del, and I'll pay more attention to where I aim my thrusts," she replied as they assumed their positions.

"What did your colleagues in the insurance office say when they saw my handiwork?", Nadia asked, extending her right leg in a kick.

"That I'm a colorful character," Del replied with a smile while dancing out of range and responding with his own awkward kick.

Wonder what he'd say if I asked him where his insurance office is located, Nadia contemplated. Why not? she concluded, circling around. "Where is your office located?" she asked, following another leg thrust.

"Right now I'm working out of my residence," Del replied after a fist thrust.

Clever, Nadia thought. Wonder what his real name is? Should be interesting penetrating his cover.

She's no dummy, Del reflected as they continued their workout.

Some twenty energetic minutes later both signaled a need to rest. "You've worn me out," Del confessed. "My conditioning pales by yours."

"I've about reached my endurance level," the woman replied. "And I feel somewhat dehydrated."

"Maybe we should replace our liquids," Del pursued. "Could I buy you a refreshment somewhere?"

Nothing bashful about this guy, she decided. "That might be nice," she said.

This is too easy, he thought. "Great. I noticed a lounge in the next block. Would that be okay?"

"Fine. I've had lunch there. Close and inexpensive. It's run by Koreans. We can practice the language."

* * *

They arrived separately in the parking lot of a Korean bar and café. Both managed unobtrusive glances at their respective vehicles, Nadia's being a 2014 silver Toyota SUV.

"Nice looking car," Nadia said, admiring Del's blue Chevy Malibu.

"Rental," Del replied.

Entering the café, Del greeted the proprietor in Korean, generating an approving smile as he led them to a corner table in the uncrowded lounge.

"What's your pleasure?" he asked Nadia who was studying the drink menu presented by a petite young Korean waitress.

"I should have a diet coke," Nadia said, "but I'm thinking of something stronger with this handsome stranger who I so brutally assaulted. It's been a long time since I had a vodka martini. You?"

"I'm kind of a beer guy, so I believe I'll settle for a Heineken," Del said, placing their order.

"Well," Nadia began, "tell me about you. What led an insurance salesman to study Korean and end up in a Tae Kwon Do studio with a black eye?"

Del laughed. "The last part is easy—I ran into a pretty lady with a dynamite punch. The other is rather monetary. I discovered a healthy market for insurance in the Korean community."

"Thanks for the compliment. Do I detect an eastern American accent?"

"You have a keen ear," he said as the waitress delivered their drinks. "Connecticut."

"Well, here's to the Connecticut Yankee," Nadia said, raising her glass.

"Slainte," Del responded with a Gaelic toast, tipping his beer glass. "How about you?" Del proceeded. "You exude international intrigue, and your job sounds fascinating."

Nadia placed her glass on the table after a generous sip. "Oh, that tastes good! My international intrigue is actually quite mundane—lots of schooling. My job does have its challenges, but I can't really talk about it for security reasons, of course."

"Of course," Del echoed. "But how did you gain so many language skills? I'm impressed."

"Guess I was born with an ear for languages. They come easily for me. And, Russia does have some good educational institutions. In addition, my grandfather was a language professor. Perhaps it runs in the family," she concluded, a shadow of sadness invading her face.

Shifting to lighter subjects, they found a shared fondness for dogs. Entertainment and sports followed as topics of conversation. Empty glasses prompted agreement on the need for refills.

Nadia's spritely sense of humor impressed Del, as did the occasional touch of her knee when she moved closer on their shared banquette.

"Maybe we should eat something," Del ventured as they finished their second round. "These drinks are pretty strong."

"Lots of food value in alcohol," Nadia giggled, holding up her empty glass. "Up to another?"

Del returned her smile. "I'll drink to that."

As they were finishing their third round, Nadia leaned back and spread her arms, projecting her upper rib cage which Del observed was quite attractive. "This has been fun," she proclaimed with a slight slurring of her words. "But maybe we should head home. It's been a long day."

"Yeah," Del agreed. "You're probably right. Thanks for the great company—and no black eye."

"You're cute," Nadia said, clinging tightly to Del's arm as they exited the lounge.

Approaching their cars, Nadia stumbled and was caught from falling by Del's quick grasp. "Maybe we should have eaten something," she said. "I'm feeling a bit woozy."

"Perhaps you shouldn't be driving," Del said. "Where do you live?"

"On Pimmit Drive, off Little River Turnpike," she said, fumbling in her purse for her car keys.

"I know the area," Del responded. "Why don't you leave your car here and I'll drive you home?"

"Oh, I hate to put you out. I can call a cab."

"No problem, Nadia. I'm staying close to there."

"What a gentleman," Nadia said, impulsively planting a moist kiss on his cheek.

As Del helped Nadia into his car, the warning of his FBI superiors flashed in his mind: "Watch out for the honey pots."

Chapter Five

FALLS CHURCH, VA

Nadia nodded off a few times during the fifteen-minute drive to her apartment, but revived when Del arrived at the entrance portico. "I'm so embarrassed," she said, searching her purse for her building entrance card. "Nice way to impress a new acquaintance."

"No need to feel embarrassed, Nadia. "Can happen to anyone. We'll just have to include food next time."

"You mean you'd risk a next time with such a person?"

"Don't be so hard on yourself. You've been a perfect lady."

"Far from perfect," Nadia sighed, starting to open her door, "but you're a real gentleman. Oh," she suddenly exclaimed, touching her forehead, "I feel dizzy. Those drinks seem to be catching up all of a sudden."

"Do you need help walking?"

"No, I think I can manage, but I'm mortified," she said, dropping her purse on the car floor.

Del studied the flustered woman. "You need assistance," he declared. "I'll park and lend a hand. Can't risk a fall."

"I feel so guilty imposing on you like this. You must have been a Boy Scout. Is this your good deed for the day?"

"In fact, I was a Boy Scout once."

"Well, you obviously remembered your training. What is the Boy Scout motto?"

"Be prepared," he replied.

Nadia's eyes flashed. "Are you prepared, Del?"

What does she mean by that? he wondered. "Hope so," he said, holding her arm as he guided her out of the car.

"Evening Ms. Rostov," the security guard greeted, eyeing Del closely as the couple walked with linked arms through the lobby. "And the same to you, Howard," she replied, leading Del to the elevator bank.

"Fifth floor," she said as they entered the car. "Apartment 501—to the right. You can leave me at the door, and thank you so much. You've been a life saver."

"My pleasure," Del said, watching her unsteady hand attempt to insert the door key.

"I'm such a disgrace," she said, dropping the key and sagging against the doorjamb.

Del quickly threw his arm around her waist to stop her fall. "Let's get you safely inside," he said, retrieving the dropped key and unlocking the door. He led her into the apartment, found the foyer light, and guided her to a living room couch.

"Oh, this is so humiliating," Nadia groaned, reclining on the maroon velvet sofa.

"May I get you something?" Del offered. "A glass of water perhaps?"

"Yes, that might help," she said, pointing to a kitchen-dining area in the neatly maintained apartment.

Filling a porcelain cup he found on the ceramic counter, Del returned to find Nadia fumbling to remove her black leather jacket. He helped free her from the garment, noting how snuggly her powder-blue cashmere sweater outlined her impressive upper torso.

"Thank you," she said, gulping the water before leaning back. Drawing her nylon-covered legs under her, she focused Del's attention to how shapely they were. "Sit next to me for a minute," she invited, patting the cushion. "You make me feel safe and secure. You've been so kind and thoughtful. I'm forever indebted."

"That's what friends are for, Nadia."

She held out her hand. "I'd like to be your friend, Del."

He grasped it, stimulated by its warmth and softness. "Friends," he confirmed as she maintained her grip. "I should be going," he said. "You probably need a good night's sleep."

"Yes," Nadia responded, releasing his hand and displaying a look of sadness. "That would be welcome. I've had trouble sleeping lately. Too much on my mind."

"Sorry to see you troubled, Nadia. Anything I can do to help?"

"Oh, you are so kind, but it's something I must work out for myself," she said, sniffling as tears began to drip from her eyes.

"Well, I've been told I'm a good listener, so I'm always available."

"Such rare kindness," she said, sobbing louder, her shoulders beginning to shake.

"Now, now," Del comforted, placing an arm around her shoulder. "Things will be better tomorrow."

Nadia snuggled closer and rested her left hand on his knee. "So kind," she murmured, circling her finger on his thigh. "Kiss me," she sighed, twisting her head to face him. Lips met and meshed. The contact was electric and escalating when Del's cell phone rang. He recognized the displayed phone number as the confidential number of his assumed employer. "Hello," he said.

"Urgent client need," a male voice responded. "The one you saw this morning wants to see you immediately." The call ended with an audible click.

"I need to go," Del told his inquisitive companion. "One of the requirements of my job is immediate response. Sorry."

Nadia nodded understanding, and released a small smile then ran her tongue over her full lips. "A taste of honey?" she asked. "Very nice. You have a talent for comforting a woman. To be continued?"

Del gazed into her penetrating eyes. "I certainly hope so," he said, rising to his feet.

Nadia didn't miss observing his trouser bulge.

"Rest easy," he said, heading for the door.

As he descended in the elevator, Del reviewed the evening's events: Overdone inebriation? Real personal problems? Genuine affection? It was a troubled young FBI agent who discovered his hastily parked car adorned with a no-parking citation. He called the cell number and received curt instructions: "Office. Eight a.m."

* * *

In apartment 501, the suddenly energized occupant carefully handled the cup Del had held, and placed it into a plastic bag. Let's see if our fingerprint experts can find out who you really are, Del Dixon.

As she slipped out of her clothes a few minutes later, she studied her body in the full-length bedroom mirror and sensed a subtle urging. It should be interesting to drain some of your mysteries, she thought, running her hands over her nubile body.

Chapter Six

TYSONS CORNER

Del arrived a few minutes before eight at the FBI satellite office.

Kevin Ryan was waiting for him. "Dutton's tear-assed," he murmured, escorting him into the ASAC's office.

Andy Dutton re-cradled the phone he had been gripping and stared at Del. "Didn't we recently have a conversation about honey pots?" he said with stern control.

"Yes, sir," Del replied.

"So, then, what in hell is the story about last night?"

"There's no real story, sir, just some little incidents of possible interest."

"And what might those 'little incidents' be, young man? You were in her apartment for forty-two minutes, and you were seen hanging onto each other as you hurried through the lobby."

"You had me tailed?"

"Not you, dummy. A suspected Russian spy who is possibly stealing top-secret information detrimental to our country from the South Korean Embassy. Remember what this case is all about?"

"Certainly I remember. I was just doing what I was instructed to do."

"So what's the story, Mr. Dickerson?"

Del related a succinct summary of his experiences, starting at the Tae Kwon Do studio.

Dutton listened attentively during Del's recitation, making random notes, then leaned back in his chair. "Three drinks? Who promoted that?"

Del pondered the question. "Mutual consent, I'd say. We were probably trying to feel each other out."

"Interesting expression," Dutton interjected.

Del smiled. "Just trying to do my job, sir. And, if I may ask, how much evidence do we have tying her to the Russkies?"

"One new segment," Dutton said, reviewing a note on his desk. "That silver Toyota she drove to the bar is the same one spotted at a recent Burke Lake meet with a known Russian courier."

"Hmm… does look kind of bad, doesn't it?" Del acknowledged. "But she seemed so sincere, and troubled. She mentioned worries about distant family problems and grandparents in Russia. Worth pursuing those angles, boss?"

Dutton paused while contemplating the question, then shook his head. "I don't know if I'm getting soft in the head, but I think we have to rely on this young character to continue the inquiry, if he can keep his pants on, Kevin. You up to it?" he challenged Del, "again pardon the expression."

Del nodded. "Yes, sir. I'm committed to a wonderful lady."

"Yes you are," Dutton replied. "I've met Anna. A special lady. Don't forget your priorities."

"Never," Del pledged before leaving the ASAC's office with Ryan.

"So what's your next contact with the woman?"

"Tomorrow night at the Tae Kwon Do studio."

"Like the boss said, be careful. Meanwhile, I suggest you again review the honey pot techniques they employ. Good to know what might be thrown at you."

* * *

BURKE LAKE PARK

Nadia Rostov's meet with her Russian Embassy contact was brief. While they sat on benches near the carousel ride waiting area, she slipped a small envelope to him. "It's all there and in the bag—his prints, Alexei. He's either dumb as they come, or smarter than we think. I believe I can find out what he knows about our operation."

"I'm sure you can, Nadia. Just save some of your persuasive talents for your homeland friends. I'll show you what Stalingrad steel means."

"Khui," (Dick) Nadia retorted, hurrying away.

* * *

From the rear of their surveillance van that had followed the courier to the park, Special Agents Curtis Oswald and Cynthia Chalmers were busily videotaping the meet. "One more confirmation," Chalmers commented to her partner.

"Yeah," Oswald responded, "and I hope you noticed the bag she arrived with."

Chalmers glared. "You don't think I missed seeing him leave with it? I didn't get out of training school yesterday, Mr. Chauvinism!"

Oswald raised his hands in surrender. "Still so touchy," he chuckled.

"Men!" Chalmers exclaimed, storing her equipment.

"Can't live without us, can you?" Oswald said, scurrying toward the driver's seat.

"What did I do to deserve a partner like you?" Chalmers questioned as the nondescript van proceeded back to the office.

Oswald grinned. "Probably pissed off Kevin with your anti-male attitude. Which makes me wonder why he stuck me with you. Rather diabolic I'd say."

"You think I have an attitude?"

"Oh, no. It's just accidental that you growl at every guy we follow."

"They're the enemy, Curt! Trying to screw our country, and perhaps kill us on the way."

"You may have a point, Cynthia, but you and I are on the same team."

"Yeah, I see your side. I'll stop barking at you."

"Thanks. By the way, I've been impressed with your investigative skills and good work habits."

"That's nice of you. Probably hangover from the military," she replied.

"What branch?"

"Air Force. I was a helicopter pilot before joining the Bureau."

"Sounds interesting. Any good stories?"

Chalmers paused, a distant look invading her face. "Some good, some not so good."

"Why'd you leave the service? You must have had a good rank."

"Captain," she answered. "It wasn't that. It was one of the not so good experiences."

"Sorry if I rekindled bad memories," Oswald said. "I fully understand if you don't want to talk about it."

"No, I'm told it's healthy to air such things. It's why I left the Air Force. It happened in Iraq. My co-pilot, Rod, and I were in a convoy, heading for our base when an IED exploded under our vehicle. Rod was killed instantly. I was wounded and temporarily blinded. Thankfully, most of my eyesight was restored, but I was unable to continue flying. That prompted me to leave, along with another painful reason." Chalmers hesitated and wiped her eyes. "Rod and I were engaged—scheduled to be married at the end of our deployments."

Oswald concentrated on his driving. "So sorry, Cynthia."

"Thanks. Another factor may have influenced my antipathy for men. Investigators subsequently identified the guy who planted the IED. He was a worker in our camp. Cook by day. Bomber by night."

"Wow, guess I can understand the bitterness. But aren't we taught to forgive our enemies?"

"You sound like a chaplain."

Oswald smiled.

"You never told me what you did before joining the Bureau," Chalmers explored.

Oswald's smile broadened. "You said I sounded like a chaplain. You were close. I was a seminarian for five years before signing up."

"You mean you were going to be a priest? I envisioned you as having a cute wife and a couple of kids. What happened?"

"My religious order and I concluded that I did not have the necessary vocation, and that we would all be better off if I pursued another career. No wife. No kids. I had Bureau friends who encouraged me to apply, assuring me that I'd fit right in with the discipline and commitment required in our job. So, after three years in Omaha, here I am, your chauvinist partner."

Chalmers leaned back and began singing, *Getting to Know You.*

"You have a nice voice," he complimented.

"And you may not be as chauvinistic as initially suspected," she said as the van rolled on.

FBI Code Name: SPYTRAP

Chapter Seven

ANNANDALE, VA

Nadia looked subdued to Del when they gathered at the beginning of the evening Tae Kwon Do session. "I apologize for the scene the other night," she said, bowing before their first match.

"No apologies needed," Del said, evading an arm jab.

"Won't happen tonight," she said, dancing away. "I'm going to church."

During a short break, Nadia elaborated. "I've joined a Russian Orthodox church in Fairfax. Have a service tonight."

"Good for you," was all that Del could think to say as they resumed the contest.

"See you soon," Nadia said as they completed the session. "Give me a call." She handed him a business card. "My personal cell number is on the back."

"Say a prayer for me," Del said as they parted.

TYSONS CORNER

Andy Dutton, Kevin Ryan and Del were in deep deliberations in Dutton's office.

"Church?" Dutton mused. "That's a new twist. What do you think, Kevin?"

Ryan rubbed his chin. "Somewhat of a surprise, but we knew from checking her background that she was a Christian."

"Working for the commies," Dutton interjected.

"Yes, and it looks like we have enough evidence to get her fired from the South Korean Embassy. Identifying that leak was our original goal, of course."

"True," Dutton agreed. "There appears to be no question she was the leak. However, it might be an opportunity to identify bigger fish in the Russkie operation."

"We could bounce a couple of their embassy attaches as persona non grata, boss, but I like the idea of trying to do more damage to their network."

"Me, too. What do you think, Del?"

"I don't have the foreign counterintelligence experience you've both had, but I agree it might be worth keeping fishing."

"You good with continuing to dangle the rod, apologizing once more for the choice of words?" Dutton asked.

Del laughed. "I like working with folks with senses of humor. Sure, it's consistent with the Bureau's missions."

"Well said," Dutton remarked. "So, what's the game plan, Kevin?"

"Keep up the contact with the woman, like we're not on to her. Feed a little innocuous misinformation to make it appear we haven't caught on. See what more we can learn about their apparatus. The espionage battle never ends, we all know."

Dutton looked at Del. "Okay with you? You said she gave you her personal number."

"Yes, sir."

"Call her then. And remember the honey traps."

"Roger, boss."

McLEAN, VA

They were seated in the top row of the IMAX theatre in the Tysons Corner mall. Alexei occupied the aisle seat, sitting next to Nadia. Three vacant seats separated Nadia from other patrons in the same row. The row in front of the pair was empty. Booming surround-sound masked their whispered conversation. Alexei had his arm draped possessively around Nadia's shoulder, huddling like lovers. "His name is Delbert Dickerson," Alexei informed. "He's an FBI Agent."

"Doesn't surprise me," Nadia replied. "They're on to us. Do we pull the plug?"

"We still don't have the key data, Nadia. We're so close. He doesn't know that we know who he is. I think we should keep trying."

"We?" Nadia said in a sarcastic tone. "Don't you mean 'me?' It's my ass on the line."

"A very nice one," Alexei replied, tightening his embrace, his warm breath invading her ear. "We need to find out how much the guy knows about us. Use your special talents. Hard for a man to resist your charms."

"Alexei, if you don't get your hand away from my crotch I'll break your fucking fingers."

"Suka," (Bitch,) Alexei growled, reeling back.

"Mudak." (Asshole) Nadia retorted, rising to leave.

FALLS CHURCH, VA

Nadia was relaxing in her apartment later that evening, watching TV and sipping on a glass of wine when her cell phone rang. "Well, hello, Del, nice of you to call."

"Hope I'm not disturbing you, Nadia. How did your church service go the other night?"

"It was enriching," she said. "How have you been?"

"Good. Busy selling insurance, but I wanted to take a break to say hello."

"You work long hours."

"Part of the job, but I'm through for the day now and I was wondering if you might be free for a nightcap in the neighborhood."

"Oh, that would be nice, but I just changed into my nightie."

"Well, perhaps another time."

"Definitely, but, if you don't mind seeing someone in a housecoat, we could still visit tonight, if you don't mind coming here."

Del gulped. Visions of honey pots formed. He thought of his mission, and of his fiancée. "Well, if it's not too much of an imposition, I can be there in twenty minutes."

Nadia smiled as she ended the call. She moved into her bedroom and changed into a black silk teddy. She sprayed a mist of Dior Pure Poison over her breasts and slipped into a lacy black robe. She examined herself in the mirror as she mused. *Looking forward to your visit, Special Agent Delbert Dickerson. Wonder what your boiling point is.*

As Nadia moved into her living room she noticed the bulletin from her new church and paused to scan the pastor's message: "I escaped the Godless regime. So can you!" Thoughts of her distant grandparents flooded her mind. *Oh, to be free. I don't want to keep doing this. How do I escape?*

Chapter Eight

Parking in a visitor's space at Nadia's apartment, Del locked his Glock automatic in his trunk and secured his credentials and badge in the glove compartment. Going in naked, he silently chuckled. This could be testy.

Howard, the same security guard on duty on his earlier visit buzzed him into the lobby, informing him that Ms. Rostov had called down to authorize admittance. "She's a special lady," the guard commented, closely studying Del. "We all like her."

I know your background, Del thought. Twenty-year Navy vet. Relax, Howard. We're on the same side. "Likewise," Del responded.

The door to apartment 501 was slightly ajar as Del prepared to knock.

"Welcome," Nadia said. "Better circumstances than last time. Please come in. Let me take your jacket."

Del buzzed her proffered cheek and shrugged off his blazer. "You are looking much more like yourself, Nadia. Your healthy glow becomes you."

"Your parents obviously trained you with good manners, my new friend."

"I'm concerned with your wellbeing, Nadia. You mentioned heavy personal problems. What can I do to help lighten your burden?"

"Let us relax first," Nadia said, moving toward a mini-bar in the corner of the living area. "I'm having chardonnay—no vodka tonight! What may I serve you?"

"The same sounds good," Del said.

Nadia half-filled a large goblet and thrust it forth. "Fruit of the vine."

"Sounds like church," Del said.

"Yes, a recent reminder of my childhood. My new pastor gives hope with his escape a few years ago from the old Soviet empire."

"We never talked much about your background," Del probed. "Is it off topic?"

Nadia took a generous sip and settled in the corner of her maroon sofa. The velvet fabric seemed to warmly embrace her black nightwear. "Not if you're willing to listen," she said. "It's been a long time since I had a listening ear."

"Just call me Dumbo," Del said with a laugh, rubbing his ear and devouring a healthy mouthful of wine. "I'm all ears."

"I know about Dumbo," Nadia said in a melodic tone. "Disney characters are big around the world, including Russia."

Del leaned forward from his overstuffed lounge chair opposite Nadia, noting the bare leg partially exposed by the parted hem of her gown. He took another sip. "Tell me about your life in Russia, and how you arrived here—a happy event I must say," he hastily added with a smile.

"I was fortunate," Nadia said after draining her glass and pouring both a refill. "My language skills, and the professional affiliations of my grandfather with associates in the United States resulted in my employment by an international translation service in Washington, D.C. That led to my current employment. My parents had been allowed to accompany me to America and life, like they say, looked rosy. Then, my world shattered when my parents were killed in a horrific auto crash on the Baltimore Beltway."

"How tragic," Del said in a comforting tone, watching Nadia struggling to maintain her composure. "What about before you came here?" he asked in an effort to divert her recollections.

Nadia pondered the question with a strained expression, before forcing a slight smile. "I had a relatively normal and happy childhood, loving parents and grandparents, good education, active in athletics, a number of jobs. Then, I was invited to participate in some government training programs—'for the better of Mother Russia' I was told. 'Your family will be proud of you' they said." She appeared to be struggling for control, on the verge of tears. "My only remaining relatives, my grandparents, are still in Russia, and have not been permitted to join me here." Tears began forming in her eyes. "I'm sounding like a simpering baby," Nadia said, wiping her eyes. "You didn't expect to find a weeping woman I'm sure," she said, refilling their glasses.

"What employment did you have in Russia?" Del explored to redirect the conversation.

Nadia's eyes flickered. "I had a variety of jobs, some quite interesting."

"Like?"

"I was a model for a few years."

"Well, you certainly fill the role," Del said with a smile. "You're a strikingly good-looking woman."

Nadia sighed. "I've been told that. It can be a burden sometimes." She pointed to an album on an adjacent table. "That's part of my portfolio." Del picked it up, reading the gold embossed title, NADIA.

"You might be shocked," she said, watching as he opened the book.

Del's attention accelerated as he viewed the artistic poses. His eyes widened. He felt his temperature rising as he turned the pages. "You must have been cold," he managed to say studying one completely nude pose by an ice sculpture.

"They had a heated tent nearby. Did you notice how the frigid air hardened my nipples?"

Del could feel his face aflame. "Yes, I noticed."

Nadia's face was flushed. "I don't have many secrets left," she said with resignation.

Del closed the album, sensing a strong urging in his groin area. "Ah… like I said, you're an exceptionally beautiful woman."

"They made me do many distasteful things," Nadia murmured. "They even had a training school for us—called it a 'Finishing School.' I'm so ashamed," she said, standing up, a movement that caused the belt of her gown to loosen and reveal parts of the flimsy garment below. She moved to Del and sat on his lap. "Do you think awful of me now?"

Del felt feverish.

"I don't want to live this life," she sobbed, wrapping her arms around Del and settling her head on his chest. "They treat me like a piece of meat. Anything for their cause!"

Del felt her tears dampening his shirt. As she wiggled in his lap he felt ready to explode.

"You don't have to do anything you don't want to do in this country," Del managed to gasp.

"But they won't let my grandparents leave Russia. They keep holding that over my head."

"That's extortion, Nadia."

Nadia snickered. "That's Russia. I'd do anything to get them out. I feel trapped and so helpless." Her trembling lips brushed Del's.

"Oh, boy," Del's stimulated brain debated. His body struggled for dominance. Her kiss seemed to be tilting the balance when the alarm sounded. "Attention!" an overhead speaker blared, followed by a recorded message. "A fire has been reported in the building. All occupants should immediately depart, using the stairways. The elevators cannot be used. Repeat," the message continued.

Nadia stood. "Another alarm! What a nuisance. There have been several lately—all false, but I guess we need to evacuate."

Saved by the bell, Del reflected while glancing at Nadia's scanty apparel. "Maybe you should grab a coat."

Nadia was already reaching into a hall closet for a raincoat. "Let's go," she said, leading a stiff-legged Del out into the crowded hallway. "We can continue our discussion later."

* * *

"Glad you don't live on the fifteenth floor," Del commented as they rode the elevator back to her floor after a twenty-minute stay in the crowded lobby.

"Another false alarm," the security guard had confirmed to Nadia. "Sorry if it disrupted your evening," he added with a glance at Del.

Enjoy your imagination, Howard, was Del's thought.

* * *

"So where were we?" Nadia asked as she removed her coat and rehung it in the closet.

"On the brink of a problem, I believe," Del said in a serious tone.

Nadia's eyebrows rose in a questioning gaze.

"I need to speak frankly," Del proceeded, taking his seat across from Nadia's sofa.

"Do we need a drink to pursue the conversation?"

"Probably better not for me, Nadia."

"I'm listening," she said. "You sound serious."

"Nadia," Del began, "I have a confession to make to you."

"Sounds like church again," she said with a light smile.

"They say it's good for the soul," Del continued. "You are a remarkably appealing woman, but I feel obligated to tell you that I'm in a committed relationship with a lovely lady out west, and have vowed to remain faithful to her."

Nadia listened without visible expression, then emitted a small chuckle. "I've heard there are such men, and now I have met one. How refreshing. I salute you."

"I'm grateful that you understand, Nadia, because I consider you a special friend who I feel is being exploited, one I want to help with her problems."

"That's nice to know, but how do you think you can help me?"

"Well, I have friends in certain circles I believe could help you under certain circumstances."

"That sounds intriguing, Del. And what might those certain circumstances be?"

Del paused. "Maybe a glass of wine might help after all."

"I agree," Nadia said. "You have my curiosity peaking," she added, pouring each of them a glass of white wine.

Del took a sip while collecting his thoughts, his mind reeling with questions on how far he could go. Where are those foreign counter intelligence pros when I need their advice, he wondered. Well, I've been trained to think for myself, so here goes. "I believe in being honest in my dealings, Nadia."

"A commendable trait," she responded.

"The friends I mentioned are in the government."

"The U. S. government?"

"Yes."

"The FBI perhaps?"

"Yes again."

Nadia took a sip from her glass and smiled. "You said you like to be honest in your dealings."

"That's correct."

"Then why did you give me a false name when we met, Special Agent Dickerson?"

Del was momentarily speechless. He placed his wine glass on a side table and stared at Nadia, his mouth agape.

She stared back. "Time for a little truth?" she asked.

Damn, looks like I royally blew this, he thought. How do I play this? "You surprise me, Nadia. I knew you were smart, but that's truly impressive. How did you find out?"

"Don't underestimate <u>my</u> associates. They're quite skilled. You left your fingerprints in my apartment. Remember the cup of water?"

Del nodded with a knowing smile. "Obviously, your associates are highly professional."

"Something that your side should remember. So, are you going to arrest me?"

"Hadn't planned on it, "Del answered. "But, now that you mentioned it, that could become a possibility."

Nadia smirked. "By my friend who lies? What other untruths have you told me?"

Del shrugged. "That's about it, except for the insurance front."

"That sounded sort of fishy from the start, Del."

"Yeah, and I'm glad you didn't offer to buy a policy."

Nadia released a small laugh. "So, as they say, shall we lay our cards on the table? Was your offer to help me get out from under their domination true, or another lie?"

"Absolutely true, Nadia."

"And getting my grandparents out?"

"Also true."

She picked up her wine glass and took a sip. "Well then, it looks like we can do business. Where do we start?"

"I believe my superiors would like a thorough debriefing by agents experienced in handling defectors."

"Never envisioned being called that," Nadia remarked in a subdued voice.

Del nodded understanding. "Probably best to do it in the nearby FBI office. We can arrange to get you there covertly. Protecting you will be of the highest priority."

"That is a real concern, Del. My old associates tend to play hard ball."

"I assure your safety, Nadia. We can put you into witness protection if it appears necessary. Meanwhile, you need to act like nothing has changed while I consult my bosses about the game plan."

Nadia ran her fingers through her hair. "This is quite a gamble."

"But a road to freedom," Del responded.

Nadia sighed. "Worth it, if I can get my grandparents out."

"I'm sure it can be arranged," Del assured.

"It'll be a major lifestyle adjustment for me," Nadia remarked as she stood and grasped Del's hand. "Come and let me show you some things," she said, leading him into her bedroom.

"Nice room," Del commented, studying the large circular bed and ceiling mirrors.

Nadia moved to a dresser and withdrew a pair of lacy black panties. See the pocket in front? Holds a C D. Used it to slip info out."

"Interesting," Del commented.

"Old and crude," Nadia said. "Vastly improved lately," she said, picking up a lipstick-sized tube. "You know where it fits" she asked with a slight sparkle in her eyes.

"Yes," Del said, feeling flushed as he inhaled the fragrant perfume engulfing the room.

"See the chandelier?" Nadia asked, pointing at the sparkling light fixture centered over the bed.

"Very elegant," Del acknowledged.

"Notice the small mirrors between the bulbs?"

"Yes, and I'm guessing that there are lenses behind them."

Nadia nodded. "High definition." A small smile emerged. "I imagine you might have photographed well."

Del began to feel aroused.

Nadia moved closer. "Is it permitted to kiss a defector goodnight?" she asked, opening her arms.

"Don't recall hearing of a rule against it," he said in compliance with the invitation.

Chapter Nine

TYSONS CORNER

ASAC Andy Dutton held his head with both hands as he slumped back in his chair at 8:30 the following morning. He turned to Supervisor Ryan who appeared similarly distressed. "He's going to get us all fired, Kevin. This is what I've been worried about. He let her know who he is and where he works."

Both looked at Del who was sitting silently across from Dutton's desk. "We both warned you about falling into a honey trap," Dutton groaned.

"With all due respect," Del said somewhat indignantly, "I didn't fall into a honey trap."

"How else would you describe it?" Dutton pressed. "You just told us you were drinking with her, and she was displaying her underwear in her bedroom next to a big circular bed. You're claiming nothing else happened?"

"Yep, and did I mention that she didn't have much on, and had showed me her modeling album with a bunch of nude shots?"

"And she didn't ply her specialty on you?"

"That's what I'm saying, sir. Not that it was easy to ignore."

Dutton took a breath. "They told me you were different. Hard for a man to resist."

"I guarantee it was hard, Mr. Dutton."

Dutton released an understanding smile. "I'm looking forward to meeting Miss Rostov. How about you, Kevin?"

Ryan nodded. "For sure."

Dutton turned back to Del. "So, when can we see the lady to discuss things?"

"Any time she's not working."

Dutton nodded. "Yes, we need to keep her in place, without her displaying any indications she is not fully committed to her mission. Think she can pull it off?"

"She's a convincing actress," Del answered.

"Okay, arrange to bring her here after dark. Use a blacked-out surveillance van, and bring her in through the dedicated elevator in the basement. You'll need some help," Dutton continued, turning to Ryan. "Who do you have available?"

Ryan paused for a moment before replying. "Oswald and Chalmers. Both sharp, with FCI experience. They've been doing some surveillances involving her, so they know the background of the case."

"Good. Put them on this full time, and start a full-press inquiry to determine how our Russian friends got access to our fingerprint files. Plug that leak without delay."

"You can bet on that, boss," Ryan assured. "Someone's ass is about to get fried."

Dutton turned to Del. "You're kind of unbelievable, but I have to acknowledge that you've provided some impressive results. A valuable defector who can possibly lead us to identifying some higher ups in their espionage network, to say nothing of identifying the leak in the South Korean Embassy. Pretty good work, Dickerson."

"Thanks, sir. I just try to do my job."

"And maintain your virtue," Ryan added with a grin.

"I promised my fiancée," Del responded. "Sure do miss her."

"Keep up the good work and you might be back together before you know it," Dutton predicted.

SAN FRANCISCO

Anna Chen was enjoying a Chinese Cultural Center fund-raising party with her Embarcadero gift shop employer. Mrs. Fong, a key organizer of the event, had invited her prized assistant to accompany her to the glittering ballroom in the Fairmont Hotel on Nob Hill. "You will attract some wealthy donors," she told the beauteous woman of American-Chinese heritage.

"Bait," Anna had teased when invited.

"No, just good business. I wouldn't let anyone harm my precious flower. I know you are faithful to that young man working back east, and notice how much you yearn for him."

"Yes, and I wonder how he is surviving the Washington temptations. He seems to have a knack for getting into trouble."

"Think positive, my dear. By the way, that new lavender sheath fits your lovely figure admirably."

"And your white satin gown with red trim is striking, Mrs. Fong. It brings back memories of our homeland."

Looks of far-away recollections briefly graced their faces. "But, we are here to raise money for worthwhile causes, Anna. Let's pay attention. They are starting the bidding for some wonderful auction prizes."

A pair of well-dressed Asian businessmen had moved close to the women, one signaling a roving waitress to deliver all of them a glass of champagne.

"Bankers," Mrs. Fong whispered to Anna after introductions were made.

Spirited bidding ensued for a variety of donated prizes.

Mrs. Fong beamed. "Our charities will again be healthy."

The men made bids on a number of items, while exchanging pleasantries with the women.

"Now for the special drawing," the auctioneer announced when the last of the donated gifts were dispersed. "You all received a red ticket when you arrived. Get it out. Someone is going to receive a wondrous surprise, generously donated by one of our strongest supporters, East-West Travel Tours."

"Wonder what it could be," Anna said, fingering her ticket.

"The special prize" the auctioneer intoned after a dramatic pause, "is a round-trip, first-class ticket on American Airlines to our nation's capital, Washington, D.C., along with five nights lodging at the Ritz-Carlton Hotel!"

Oh's and ah's sounded in the ballroom.

"And," the auctioneer announced in a vibrant voice, "the winning number is 5 1 7 6 3!"

Anna studied her ticket. "That's me!" she shrieked, feeling ready to collapse.

"Wonderful," Mrs. Fong exclaimed, hugging Anna.

"More champagne," one of the bankers called to a waitress. "We must toast our lucky winner."

"Won't Del be surprised?" Anna said in her dazed excitement. "It appears some of his fabulous luck has touched me."

Chapter Ten

TYSONS CORNER

They were seated around a large conference table in the Northern Virginia satellite office of the Washington Field Office. Del sat next to Nadia. Across the well-polished blonde oak table were ASAC Andy Dutton, Supervisor Kevin Ryan, and Special Agents Cynthia Chalmers and Curtis Oswald.

"I look outnumbered," Nadia remarked. "Do I need an attorney to protect my interests?"

Dutton smiled. "I don't think so, Ms. Rostov. I believe we are all on the same side, and we appreciate what you are doing. Let me introduce my associates." When he came to Oswald, the agent greeted her in Russian. "Dobroye utro," he said.

Nadia's eyes sparkled. "You speak my native language beautifully. And good morning to you. You don't look Russian."

"Courtesy of the Armed Forces Foreign Language Institute in Monterey, California," Oswald explained. "The same place that educated Del in Korean."

Nadia gazed at Del. "They must have good instructors, along with good students. I've been impressed with Del's talents."

"So have we," Dutton remarked with a knowing smile. "So, shall we get down to the business at hand?"

An hour later decisions had been reached about Nadia's role, and Cynthia was showing Nadia how the miniature recorder could be concealed in her panties.

DULLES INTERNATIONAL AIRPORT, VIRGINIA

Their greeting at the American Airlines arrival lounge was exhilarating as they embraced like the long-apart lovers they were. "Oh, you feel so good," Anna breathed into Del's ear as they hugged enthusiastically.

"Nowhere as wonderful as you, Anna. And you have reminded me of just how beautiful you are."

"Are you saying you'd forgotten how much I love you? Have those Washington temptresses faded your memory?"

Del released his embrace and looked into his fiancée's eyes. "Never," he proclaimed, watching the baggage carousel start to rotate with an array of look-alike luggage. "You're one in a million," he said, spotting Anna's burgundy-colored suitcase with dangling gold ribbon approaching them. "See, you're just like your suitcase. You stand out above all the rest."

"Aren't we lucky?" she said, watching Del grab her bag and lead her out of the terminal. "I can't wait for you to tell me what you've been doing."

WASHINGTON, D.C.

The deluxe room on the seventh floor of the Ritz-Carlton Hotel harbored the heady scent of feverish lovemaking. "Whew," Anna said, brushing her matted black hair from her moist forehead. "Appears you have been long deprived."

"I believe you've just seen how much," Del exhaled in a satisfied tone as his head nestled against hers on the oversize satin pillow.

"I'm glad our separation was only brief. You seemed ready to explode."

"I think I just did," Del chuckled, running his fingers over Anna's flushed cheeks.

"Yes," Anna concurred, caressing his back. "I noticed."

"You certainly provide luxurious surroundings, Ms. Chen. Weren't we blessed with your lucky number?"

"You're my lucky number, my dear. And, I do believe I've inherited some of the renowned Del Dickerson luck. I can't wait for what happens next."

"Me, too. I have an important meeting in the morning about the direction of our case."

"Then we better get some sleep," Anna said, snuggling closer.

"Sleep?" Del questioned.

"Taiwanese humor," Anna said, reaffixing her generous lips.

TYSONS CORNER

Coffee and donuts were being avidly consumed at the scheduled nine a.m. conference. Supervisor Kevin Ryan presided. Nadia was accompanied by Curtis Oswald and her new companion, Cynthia Chalmers. Del arrived a minute before the start.

"You look like you slept in your clothes on a park bench," Ryan commented to Del.

Del's crooked smile signaled no comment.

"Oh," Ryan announced, "I just recalled that Del's fiancée arrived last night from California. That might explain things."

"She won an airline ticket to Washington," Del explained.

Nadia's eyes twinkled. "Lucky lady. I look forward to meeting her."

"All in good time," Ryan spoke up. "Right now, we have important business to explore."

The next thirty minutes were some of the most illuminating in Del's recent memory. "So," he said after listening attentively to Ryan's presentation, "we dangle Nadia as supplier of the missing link." He looked at Nadia. "Are we being fair?"

Ryan spoke with authority. "The risk has been explained to her."

Nadia broke in. "I understand the danger. The expectation of freedom for me and my grandparents is worth it. I'm in completely."

Del looked at her with admiration. "I've seen her in action. She's tough!"

Ryan turned to Oswald and Chalmers. "To insure that this team is on the same page, let's clarify our goals so no one is in doubt. We're going to be imbedded like family for a while." His associates listened as he proceeded. "Thanks to the good work of Nadia and Del, we have cleared the intelligence leak problem at the South Korean Embassy. Score one for the home team!"

With a crooked smile, Del raised his right fist in feigned celebration.

Ryan picked up. "That was the easy part. Now it gets hairy. We need to keep Nadia seemingly gathering the sought for data so we can learn identities of others on the transmission line. We know she's been working for the Russians, and they're selling the information to the North Koreans. The NK's are desperate to get the lacking technology for one of their intercontinental missile guidance systems threatening us and their neighbors. They've already managed to get some critical data from international high-tech firms. It's high stakes, folks."

"This is a lot more complicated than I thought when I was invited aboard," Cynthia Chalmers commented.

"It's really simple," Ryan responded with a smile. "All we need to do is outsmart one of the most skilled espionage systems in the world; keep our prized asset safe; and deny a rogue nation means to blow up the universe." He paused and surveyed his audience. "You've all been well trained, and have been hand-picked. We know you're the best. Just do your jobs and we'll be fine."

Ryan waited a few beats more before releasing a small smile. "While we're evading disaster, I believe it might be satisfying to gift them a little remembrance, perhaps in the form of a tiny bit of undetectable misinformation that just might mess up the guidance brains of their missiles."

"Right on!" Del exclaimed. "They've had major failures before."

Ryan grinned. "The Lab and tech folks have been working on it for a while. Boom!" he said with an upraised thumb.

Nadia gazed admiringly at Ryan. "Your agency appears to know what it is doing, not exactly the bumbling bureaucrats some critics have painted you as."

"We try," Ryan said with an appreciative nod. "And we all need to keep giving the case our best shots, and maintain the appearance that nothing has changed the status quo. When do you next meet Alexei Nikolay?"

"Tomorrow, at Burke Lake Park, three p.m."

"Tell him you're hoping to learn something about the missile code after a meeting at the Embassy of some space engineers. Cynthia and Curt will discreetly cover the meet at the park. See if you can get him talking about the info search. Let's see how the concealed listening device works. You okay with that?"

"Yes, it's more comfortable than other devices I've experienced."

"And see if you can find out how they got into our fingerprint files to identify Del as an agent."

"We haven't pinned that down yet?" Del asked.

"They're proceeding delicately, I'm told," Ryan answered. "They identified the immediate source, a young female file clerk in the Montgomery County P.D., but want to see who else is in the chain before they bring it all down. Just a matter of time. Lots of facets to attend to, speaking of which, I believe we need to maintain the facade of Del and Nadia's Tae Kwon Do activity, in case anyone is watching. Do you have a session planned?"

Nadia spoke up. "Tonight, if Del can tear himself away from his west coast amour."

Ryan looked at Del.

"Sure," Del said. "Part of the job."

Nadia smiled. "I won't disable him completely."

Chapter Eleven

ANNANDALE, VA

"You look tired," Nadia greeted Del at the beginning of their evening session at the martial arts studio. "Would you like a less aggressive partner to practice with tonight? I wouldn't want to exhaust your energies."

"No, I'm familiar with you," Del replied.

Nadia smirked. "Not that familiar, remember? Nadia isn't often denied."

Geez, is she going to hold that against me, Del wondered as they bowed to start a bout.

Wham! A sharp kick to his right shin signaled she apparently did.

"Sorry," she said, circling around him. "Guess my timing is off."

Del tried to move out of further reach as Nadia seemed to display extra vigor in her movements, grazing his left arm with a rigid fist.

"Sorry again, hope it doesn't leave a bruise," she said, spinning away.

"You seem a bit agitated," Del managed to say as he barely escaped another sharp leg kick.

"You should see me when I'm really agitated," Nadia said as their match ended.

"Have I offended you, Nadia? I thought we were friends."

Nadia paused and lowered her eyes. "You're right. I've been acting childish, taking out my frustrations on you. I owe you an apology." She fixed her eyes on his. "Please forgive my boorish behavior. Friends?" she added, extending her right hand.

"Friends," Del agreed with a comforting handshake.

"Good," Nadia said as they commenced another bout, this one markedly less combative.

Twenty minutes later they were walking out of the studio, heading for their parked cars. "Enjoy the rest of the evening," she said before starting her engine and spinning her wheels as she sped away.

Del shook his head. Women are sure hard to understand sometimes, he reflected as he slid behind the wheel and headed for the Ritz-Carlton.

* * *

Anna and Del enjoyed a tasty dinner at the Old Ebbitt Grill before returning to their upscale hotel. She spoke with enthusiasm about her bus sightseeing tour of Washington while he was at work, and asked how his day had gone.

"We had an in-depth conference about the case I'm working one," he replied, "but I can't discuss details, you know."

"Oh, I'm well aware of that," Anna said, beginning to undress. "I certainly don't want to pry. I hope my presence isn't interfering with your performance of duty."

"No way, Anna. I'm thrilled you're here. It was kind of Mrs. Fong to give you the time off."

"She's a wonderful boss. She said to convey her regards, and remind you to behave yourself."

"A good watchdog," Del said with a laugh. "Tell her I'm behaving admirably."

"I'm sure of that," Anna said, continuing to disrobe. "Have you met anyone interesting at your Tae Kwon Do class?"

"Well, since you mention it, I have. It's part of my assignment. But I can't talk about it, of course."

"Of course," she agreed, watching Del remove his undershirt. "Are those bruises on your arms?" Anna asked with alarm.

Del peered at the discolorations. "The classes sometimes get physical," he said.

"Well, tell the guy who wounded my fiancée he'll be in trouble if he does it again."

"I'll pass on the message," Del said, leading his naked lover to the gurgling Jacuzzi tub.

TYSONS CORNER

"Hey, we have an investigative opportunity," Kevin Ryan said as he greeted Del the following morning. "There's a big reception tomorrow night at the South Korean Embassy. Should be a lot of cyberspace lobbyists looking to make a deal. We might identify others trying to compromise our security ties with our friends, as well as anyone appearing to be a danger to Nadia."

"Will she be there?"

"Definitely, she's their prime translator, after all."

"Sounds logical," Del agreed. "How do we find out what occurs?"

"You provide us a comprehensive report."

"Me?"

"Right. Who better to know what to look for? You speak the language, are aware of the problem, and might encounter some worthwhile sources."

"Yeah, I can see the possibilities, Kevin. Do I need an invitation?"

"Already arranged by our Embassy contacts. And it's good for a guest. Might you have anyone in mind?"

"Anna!" Del immediately replied. "She'll fit right in."

Ryan smiled. "You catch on fairly fast. Dutton and I already concluded that."

"She'll be delighted," Del said. "She's been feeling sort of out of the action. She has helped the Bureau in several cases, you know."

"Yes, we know," Ryan laughed. "Dutton said she'll probably save your ass again. He's high on your lady."

"Not as high as me," Del said with a grin. "I need to get back to the Ritz-Carlton and inform her. She was just awakening from the feather bed. We have only a couple of nights left there."

"Tough duty," Ryan snickered.

"Yeah," Del concurred. "The Jacuzzi water was a little tepid last night. Need to get the hotel engineer working on that."

Ryan rolled his eyes. "Dutton said you're a special case."

Chapter Twelve

WASHINGTON, D.C.

"Wonderful!" Anna squealed when Del broke the news. "I can't wait to see who we might meet."

Should be interesting, Del thought, thinking of Nadia.

"What will I wear?" Anna wondered. "I need to go shopping."

"Have fun," Del responded. "I need to get back to the office. There's an important meeting this afternoon."

BURKE LAKE PARK

"Right on time," Cynthia Chalmers commented to her partner as she peered out the one-way windows of their surveillance van at Alexei Nikolay who was approaching Nadia, seated at a remote picnic table.

"We'll soon find out how well the mic works," Curtis Oswald remarked, keeping his binoculars fixed on the pair.

* * *

"Do you have the vital data for me?" Alexei Nikolay was heard by the concealed mic to ask Nadia. "Our superiors are getting very impatient."

"Almost," Nadia replied. "I hope to have something any day."

"You said that the last time we met. Have you learned anything from the FBI agent?"

"Not much. I don't think he's very bright."

"Do you think he's on to you?"

"No, like I said, he's sort of a bumbler."

"Have you employed your special talents?"

"Alexei, I will inform you of what I learn from my efforts, but it's none of your business how I gather the information."

"Well, I don't know about that, Nadia. We all know how you've been trained. So don't pull that 'none of my business' crap. We expect you to deliver. It's your duty, and you've been well paid."

"And you have certain leverage in our homeland to insure my compliance, right?"

"Your relatives are safe and well. They depend on your performance. Do it!"

"It's not as easy as you think."

Nikolay snorted. "Do you think it was easy to get into the FBI's fingerprint files?"

"I give you credit for that," Nadia said. "How did you manage that?"

Nikolay looked self-satisfied. "Slipping a mole into that fortress took a lot of work. They keep trying to do the same to us, you know."

"I know it's an ongoing game," was Nadia's answer.

"High stakes," Nikolay said, concluding their meet. "Recline and enjoy," he said in a mocking tone before hurrying away.

"Khui!" (Prick) Nadia yelled at the departing courier.

* * *

"Their conversation came across loud and clear," Chalmers commented in the surveillance van.

"Yeah, particularly his mention of 'a mole in the fortress.' That should stir Ryan's and Dutton's juices."

"Sounded to me like more than the Maryland P.D. clerk they identified as handling Del's fingerprint inquiry, Curt. Might mean she had help from someone in Clarksburg."

"I agree that's a good possibility, but they have good internal security controls there. I toured that facility in wild, wonderful West Virginia. Tight! I believe they can pinpoint who handled Del's prints there."

"I need to put that place on my bucket list. Sounds like a fortress."

"Bring walking shoes. It's massive and houses an array of services beyond fingerprints under the title of CJIS, which I'm sure you know from your Bureau indoctrination stands for Criminal Justice Information Services Division. Guess that's why they call it CJIS. It has over 35,000 employees."

"Well then, our little mic seems to have paid off, Curt. And Nadia sounded like she had things under control. What did she call him?"

Oswald smiled. "Sort of a Russian term of endearment—loosely translated, a prick. Got to admire the lady under the pressure she faced. What next?"

"We meet with the brave lady, retrieve the equipment—that's my job— and review what else she may have observed in Markov's behavior."

"Where? Is she coming to the office again?"

"No, Kevin thought that could be too risky so he borrowed Del's hotel room key—save the Bureau the cost of renting another room. Del's not using it for a couple more days since he's been living it up with his fiancée at the Ritz-Carlton."

Oswald started the van. "That guy sure seems to live a charmed life."

FALLS CHURCH, VA

Nadia was resting atop the queen-sized bed in Del's fourth-floor room in the Westin Hotel near Tysons Corner.

"How do you think I did," she asked Cynthia who had just retrieved the hidden mic.

"You did fine, and the equipment worked well."

"And your probing about Del's fingerprint leak was excellent." Oswald observed. "It should help plug that weakness."

"Ah, everyone's probing for weaknesses, aren't they?" Nadia replied.

"That sounds philosophical," Oswald remarked.

"I studied a lot of philosophy at one time," Nadia said.

"Me too," Oswald replied. "We should compare notes."

Nadia turned on her pillow. "Any time," she said, turning her head again, inadvertently depositing a smear of lipstick on the bed pillow. "Oops, I hope Del doesn't mind. Maybe housekeeping will take care of it before he returns. Sorry about that."

"I wouldn't worry about it. Just another example of human weakness."

"Thanks for the understanding," Nadia said with a laugh. "We all have shortcomings, don't we?"

"Most definitely," the former seminarian agreed as they prepared to leave the room. "Shortcomings, but forgiveness too," he added.

"I like your attitude," Nadia said as they departed.

Chapter Thirteen

WASHINGTON, D.C.

The glittering ballroom of the South Korean Embassy on Massachusetts Avenue buzzed with conversations and tinkling cocktail glasses. Well-dressed men and women exchanged greetings and gossip as neatly groomed servers circulated with trays of tempting appetizers. Perimeter bars dispensed libations of choice, the consumption of which seemed to directly escalate the noise level.

"This seems like the old days," Anna remarked to Del with a mild look of nostalgia gracing her exotic features. "I used to accompany the Chairman to many such events."

Del was immediately reminded of his introduction to Anna in the FBI's SHARKS investigation, a major inquiry into commodities fraud where Anna's patron, a powerful United States Senator, who doggedly retained the title of Chairman even after his party lost its majority, was a key conspirator. He recalled how the Senator had sponsored Anna's entry into the country with promises of helping her locate her father, a former U.S. Army sergeant who had been ordered home before learning he had left an expectant mother behind. Del grimaced internally when he thought of how diabolically the Senator had exploited Anna before he was killed in a horrendous traffic accident while trying to flee apprehension by the FBI after his infamous fraud scheme collapsed. The ensuing romance between Del and Anna was a happier reminder, as he recalled their shared experiences in major FBI cases where Anna played a key role.

Del was jolted back to reality from his mental meanderings by Anna's announcement, "I see someone from the past."

"Where?" Del asked, turning in the direction Anna was looking.

"The man in the grey suit. He was one of the Chairman's associates before the SHARKS investigation."

"I thought we put all the bad guys in jail," Del commented. "Maybe some were missed, or he's out of jail. Let's find out. He's headed our way."

"Anna!" a florid-faced middle-aged man declared as he approached. "What a sight for sore eyes. You look as beautiful as ever."

"Hello," Anna replied. "I recognize your face, but I'm afraid I don't recall your name."

"Jason Walters from New Jersey," the man replied. "Congressman Jason Walters."

"Oh, yes. I met you once with the Chairman. Let me introduce my companion, Del Dickerson." The men shook hands.

"That was a shock about losing the Chairman. I know you were close. My condolences."

"Thanks. It was a sad event."

"What are you doing now, Anna? Why are you here?"

"Just visiting my friend," she said cautiously. "I live in California now."

"Well, it was good seeing you," Walters said, moving in the direction of the bar.

"Interesting," Del said. "I need to check him out. Is he one who got away? I thought we nabbed all the crooks involved in the Chairman's scheme."

"Speaking to him brought back memories," Anna said. "I vaguely recall meeting him at a country club in Maryland after one of the Chairman's golf outings with legislators and lobbyists. He was pretty drunk, foul-mouthed and generally nasty—a rather chilling reminder of the past."

"Past history," Del said, glancing across the room at a striking woman in a clinging red dress. Nadia.

"There's someone you need to meet," Del told Anna, nodding in Nadia's direction. "By the way, she may know me by a different name. I'll explain later."

Let's get it over with, Del told himself.

Nadia spotted them and excused herself to head in their direction.

"Well hello, Mr. Dixon. I'm delighted to see you here. Who's your guest?"

"I'd like you to meet my fiancée, Anna Chen."

"A pleasure," Nadia said as the women exchanged handshakes. "Lovely dress," Nadia added, admiring Anna's golden sheath with oriental trim. "Hoping to sell some insurance tonight?" she asked Del with a light laugh.

Anna looked with puzzlement at Del. What's going on?

Should have prepped Anna better, Del admonished himself.

"Never know where you find someone in need," Del said with a laugh.

"He's a good Tae Kwon Do partner," Nadia said. "Fast on his feet."

Have some explaining to do, Del concluded. "A worthy opponent," he said.

"Well, enjoy yourselves. I need to see if my employers need some translation help."

Anna's normal smile had disappeared. "We need to talk, Delbert."

Delbert! Oh boy. "How about a cocktail, Anna?"

"That might help," she said coldly. "You can get a glass of white wine for me while I go to the lady's room."

En route to the bar, Del passed Nadia who turned from a conversation and whispered, "Lovely lady, but she looks a little stressed."

"Thanks a lot for the help," Del replied.

As a bartender poured two glasses of wine a few minutes later, Del noticed Anna being stopped by the New Jersey Congressman.

* * *

"It was wonderful seeing you," Walters told Anna. "I've often thought about you and wondered if you needed some comforting."

"I'm very happy in my life, Jason."

"My old colleague told me how accomplished you were in comforting him."

Anna's face flushed. "That's very personal, and frankly, quite rude."

Walters edged closer, his alcohol-scented voice low. "I can reduce your tensions, Anna. Give me a call," he said, pressing a business card into her hand.

"And why would I want to do that, Congressman?"

Walters's expression was arrogant. "Maybe because I know something about your background you'd like to keep private. And, I know some juicy details about the Chairman's activities. Some of them include you. Think about it. We could make a beautiful team."

"You're a nasty man," Anna said, close to tears as she searched the room for Del.

* * *

"What happened?" Del asked, seeing Anna's devastated expression.

Anna related the conversation with Walters.

"That bastard!" Del exclaimed, his eyes darting around the ballroom. "I'm going to straighten him out."

"No, let's leave. I don't feel well, and we have a number of items to discuss."

Chapter Fourteen

WASHINGTON, D.C.

Tears flowed from Anna's brown eyes as she huddled in Del's arms in a plush love seat in their Ritz-Carlton room. "That horrible man opened so many old wounds," she sobbed.

"I should have punched him out," Del mused.

"And get yourself fired, or ruin your investigation?"

"Well, there needs to be some retribution for the hurt he caused you. What do you think he meant about juicy details about the Chairman's activities?"

Anna shook her head. "There were so many questionable activities the Chairman was involved in, separate from the commodities fraud."

"Yeah, we'll definitely look into it. The guy is a real skunk, but he does appear to have some redeeming qualities."

"Like what?" Anna queried.

"An eye for beauty. He thinks you're pretty hot."

"Ugh. Who would want to be romanced by him?"

"No one without a reason."

"You mean like an enticement to uncover what he knows?"

"That's a possibility. You're thinking like an investigator. I believe it warrants discussing with the Bureau brains."

"Baiting the hook?" she asked, settling into Del's arms. The tears had ended.

"Might be a way to catch another shark, Anna."

"I've always enjoyed working with you on your cases, Del. We've had fun."

"And success. Let me discuss it with Kevin and Mr. Dutton."

"I feel a lot better, Del, but need a cleansing shower after being touched by that horrid man."

"Need your back washed?"

"Lots of places I can't reach."

"Let me help," Del volunteered.

TYSONS CORNER

Del, Kevin Ryan, and ASAC Andy Dutton were in deep discussion behind the closed door of Dutton's impressive office. Trophies from marksman contests lined the credenza behind his tidy desk.

"We need to educate Kevin on the SHARKS special, Del. He didn't transfer in here until that thriller went down. I gave him a quick rundown, but why don't you add your recollections, including the involvement of Ms. Chen."

"Seems like yesterday," Del began, "but not to be forgotten. The case began on a scheme directed by the former Chairman of a powerful Senate Committee, and involved legislation on crop commodities for Midwest farmers that would have cost taxpayers millions of dollars. The deal included several Congressmen and Senators, and some unsavory lobbyists."

Dutton interjected a chuckle. "One of whom Del rescued from drowning in the Potomac River. He provided an entry into the conspiracy. Pardon the interruption, but I was reminded of how this guy always seems to be in the middle of the action. Go ahead, Del."

Del resumed with a smile at the memory. "The water was cold. Anyway, the investigation culminated in the arrest of the perps on a luxurious yacht off the coast of Atlantic City in a HRT drop from helicopters. Caught them with the payoff loot. Pretty dramatic."

"I heard about that," Ryan said. "Didn't you have a female agent working undercover as a chorus girl in one of the casinos?"

"Right, a former Radio City Music Hall Rockette," Dutton affirmed. "A lovely lady, I recall. And, didn't you rappel onto the boat from a helicopter, Del?"

"Yeah, and I was scared shitless."

"It was a major FBI success," Dutton added, nodding to Del to proceed.

"The case had a violent ending," Del continued. "After the Chairman was arrested he tried to escape from the Atlantic City R.A. with his share of the payoff money. He forced Anna to accompany him in his government Cadillac, with Bureau agents in hot pursuit. Speeding the wrong way on an Interstate he smashed head on into the front of a casino bus, killing him instantly. His hostage, Anna, was critically injured but survived."

"She is a gallant survivor," Dutton declared.

Del nodded in agreement. "We have become very close, Kevin. In case you don't know the background, she had been sponsored into the U.S. by the Chairman on false promises, and shamelessly exploited by him. She has subsequently played key roles in recovering some of the Chairman's hidden loot in the Bureau's CULTURED PEARL Special, where she became targeted for assassination by international gem and bomb part smugglers."

"Wow, she sounds like Superwoman," Ryan remarked with admiration.

"That's not all," Del continued. "She just recently helped the Bureau again in the DEADLY DECEPTION special at the Language School in Monterey. She was kidnaped and almost killed by a psycho in that case."

Dutton turned back towards Ryan. "And guess who was there to help her survive?"

Del smiled modestly. "We were lucky, and blessed. We are engaged, you know."

"Like I keep telling you, Kevin, this guy has more luck and lives than nine cats."

"Is that an adequate summary, Mr. Dutton?"

"Well done, Del. You've turned a lot of hair grey, but I must admit it's never dull with you around, so, concentrating on the present, we need to decide on how to proceed with Congressman Walters, along with Nadia Rostov's double-agent role."

"And Anna Chen's possible utilization again," Ryan added. "We should hire her."

Dutton looked at his watch. "I need to leave for the Hoover Building. Have a scheduled meeting with a couple of Assistant Directors about our basket of goodies. They need reminding of what goes on in our little world."

WASHINGTON, D.C.

"What now?" Anna asked from a corner of the steaming Jacuzzi in their Ritz-Carlton suite. "I'm getting spoiled from this high living."

"You don't look spoiled to me," Del replied, brushing his right toe against her thigh. "I'd describe you as pretty ripe and tender."

"I feel a bit wrinkled—all this warm water."

Del laughed. "At least it's warm. I was reminded this morning at our strategy conference of my dip into the Potomac during the SHARKS special."

"That was before I met you. Do you remember our meeting?"

"An indelible memory, Anna. Love at first sight, as the saying goes. I knocked on the door of your Georgetown townhouse. The steps were wet and slippery."

"And you slipped, and I dragged you inside for first aid."

"That was the beginning of our love, Anna. It has only gotten better."

"We've been through a lot together, Del. Like it was destiny. I'm yours in all ways, you know."

"You've helped me in so many ways, I hesitate to ask you to place yourself in jeopardy again."

"You mean pursuing the invitation of that terrible congressman?"

"Yeah, that was one of the things we discussed at today's conference."

"I'm willing, if it helps you and the Bureau."

"You should be an agent, Anna. I don't know anyone who has produced better results."

"I'm just happy to be at your side. Tell your bosses I'm available."

"You're not at my side now," he teased.

"Easily corrected," she said, moving to him. "Like I said, I'm yours in all ways."

"Prove it," he said, opening his wet arms.

She did.

FBI Code Name: SPYTRAP

Chapter Fifteen

WASHINGTON, D.C.
J. Edgar Hoover FBI Building

ASAC Andy Dutton was in the office of Assistant Director Wayne Jackson on the fifth floor of the massive FBI headquarters. "You have a nice view," Dutton said, gazing out across Pennsylvania Avenue at the Department of Justice Building.

"You could have one just as nice," Jackson said, "if you didn't keep declining further administrative advancement."

"I love field work, Wayne."

"I know what you mean," the trim black Administrator commented. "That's where the action is. I admire the way you have managed to keep the Director from promoting you up and out."

"He kept his promise after I was shot in that Detroit raid. Told me I could stay wherever I wanted. He's kept his word."

"And you've repaid it with the major cases you've handled out of the Tysons Corner satellite office."

"Glad you Headquarters folks have noticed. I have a team of top-notch personnel."

"Oh, we've noticed, particularly with what you reported on the South Korean Embassy leak investigation. I'm working with the foreign intelligence people in their Division on that matter, but my Division has the white collar fraud jurisdiction involving the New Jersey Congressman. How did he slip through the net when the SHARKS case went down?"

"I've questioned everyone who worked that case, and double-checked all the file references without luck. He must have been just outside the fringes of that action, but we're taking a closer look now, particularly with the help of the late Chairman's protégé, Anna Chen."

Jackson nodded. "I've been briefed on her remarkable assistance to the Bureau, and her affiliation with her unusual partner, Special Agent Dickerson. He sounds like a genuine character."

"He's all of that, and more," Dutton said with a grin. "Hard to describe, but somehow effective as hell."

"A rainmaker, I surmise. Anyway, in regard to the purpose of our meeting, you have full approval to pursue the Walters inquiry, and whatever other derelictions you uncover, and to employ the volunteer talents of Ms. Chen in any appropriate manner. I'll back you all the way."

"Thanks, Wayne. You live up to your reputation as a stand-up guy, like you did playing football at Syracuse."

"Wish I could run like that these days. The old knees aren't what they used to be."

"Well, if they're still up to social maneuvering, I'm having a pool-party cookout at my residence Sunday, and would love to have you and your wife see how we relax in Northern Virginia on our time off. My place is just off Old Georgetown Pike in Great Falls. Five p.m. Pool's heated. Bring your suits if so inclined. I'm inviting the cast of characters we talked about today, so you'll have a chance to personally size them up."

"Sounds like an invitation that shouldn't be declined. See you Sunday."

TYSONS CORNER

"Green lights all the way," Dutton cheerfully informed his favorite subordinate when he returned from his Headquarters' meetings.

Ryan beamed. "I know you're a good salesman, boss. Did it take much arm twisting?"

"Not really. The wheels there have all been in the field, so they recognize a serious case when they see it. Assistant Director Jackson and the foreign intelligence folks have pretty much given us carte blanche to pursue the whole schmear."

"Lots of balls in the air, boss."

"No question, and I'm depending on you to keep them bouncing. We need to insure that our group is on the same page and not tripping over each other. We're working a double-agent against the Russkies, and planning to direct a fragile source at an apparently crooked Federal legislator. We need to avoid jeopardizing the welfare of either of our operations while not antagonizing the Legislative branch. Some of them are still smarting over the embarrassment of the SHARKS exposure."

"Walking on eggshells," Ryan commented.

"Definitely, Kevin. The team must work closely together, always alert to the impact on each other. To that end, I'm inviting them all to my place Sunday, so they can establish a rapport. I'll let you extend the invitations. Casual. Five p.m. Bring bathing suits if desired. Pool's heated. I'll cook the burgers."

"Sounds like a plan, boss."

WASHINGTON, D.C.

"Well, good bye Ritz-Carlton, hello Westin," Del said, zipping his tote bag. "Our stay here is up."

"I'll miss our little Paradise Island," Anna said as she finished packing her suitcase.

"Sort of like an advance honeymoon," Del replied. "It's been great."

"We seem to do things out of order, Del. The wedding usually comes first."

Del nodded. "We were about ready for the big event in San Francisco when I was sent here."

"So we postponed the date," Anna said. "And then I came here, and we're working together on another case. Maybe we should take time out to get married, unless you are having second thoughts."

"Absolutely not, Anna. I just want to do it right, when we're not in the midst of a big case. We need to be focused on our challenges."

"Marriage is a challenge," Anna was reminding Del when his cell phone signaled a text message.

"Guess what?" he said. "Dutton's having a cookout at his home on Sunday. Everyone involved in the project will be there. You'll be able to meet all the players."

"That should be fun. Will the Russian girl be there?"

"Gee, I imagine so. She's a major player."

"Seems so," Anna said, grabbing her jacket.

FALLS CHURCH, VA

Nadia had just read her texted invitation on the secure cell phone provided by Ryan when her other cell phone rang. The conversation was brief, with no names mentioned, but she recognized the voice of Alexei Nikolay. "I'm getting heavy pressure. We need to meet at the usual place Sunday."

"Can't," Nadia replied. "Make it Monday. I'll be in church Sunday."

"Suka," (Bitch) the caller swore before hanging up.

Nadia studied her reflection in a wall mirror. Need to be careful, she told herself. She then reached for a bottle of vodka and poured herself a double shot.

Chapter Sixteen

GREAT FALLS, VA

"Man, this looks rich!" Curt Oswald said to his passengers as they traveled the long entrance drive to an impressive white brick rambler nestled in towering pine trees. "Did Dutton rob a bank?"

"Not quite," Cynthia Chalmers answered from the passenger seat. "Scuttlebutt has it that his wife inherited it from her parents who were early pioneers in the area when the land wasn't so expensive. Dutton renovated it extensively when he was transferred here and it's now a showplace."

"Capitalist pig," Nadia shouted jocularly from the snug back seat.

"See what happens in America?" Oswald joked back. "One of these can be yours one day, Nadia."

"I'd be happy in a shack if my grandparents were here with me," she said in a serious tone.

"And we're committed to that, Nadia. Now let's relax and enjoy Dutton's hospitality."

"Look, there's Kevin Ryan," Cynthia said, "getting out of his Corvette. Guess he came alone. Sporty car."

"And there's Del and Anna going into the house," Oswald pointed. "He's known as a fun guy."

"I know," Nadia said, sliding out of the snug back seat of Oswald's Buick Cascada convertible.

The arrivals were greeted by Andy Dutton and his blonde wife, Lydia, an attractive woman around fifty who exuded warmth and friendliness. "We are so pleased that you were able to join us today," she said following introductions. "Just make yourselves at home. You can change in the pool house if you brought suits. If you didn't, you'll have to wait for darkness," she said with a laugh. "Del and Anna are already headed for the pool. Kevin's in charge of the bar, and my wonderful husband is the cook. Enjoy."

"How could we not?" Oswald said as the group dispersed.

* * *

"We've spent a lot of time in water recently," Del observed to Anna as they lazily floated around the pool.

"This is warmer and calmer than our time on Chesapeake Bay when we almost drowned," Anna said, recalling their near disaster when their catamaran was destroyed in a sudden storm.

"Yes, that was an exciting way to end the CULTURED PEARL case. It seems there's always something dramatic at the conclusion of your cases, Del. You tend to attract excitement, perhaps like the woman who just came out of the pool house in that almost invisible garment."

Del looked cautiously. "It does look a little sparse," he agreed as Nadia posed momentarily at the edge of the pool before plunging in.

"Hello," Nadia greeted seconds later as she surfaced next to them. "Isn't this a splendid way to have sun and fun?"

"Couldn't be better," Del declared.

"Nice to see you again," Anna managed to say before Nadia paddled away.

Kevin Ryan was next in the pool, propelling his muscular body into the water and demonstrating powerful strokes.

"He was a Navy SEAL," Del informed Anna who nodded understandingly.

"Impressive," she said.

Curt Oswald and Cynthia Chalmers followed, both looking fit and trim, and the pool soon bubbled with enthusiastic swimmers enjoying brief respites from their serious daily demands.

"I believe we have gathered a happy group," Dutton was commenting to his wife when Assistant Director Wayne Jackson and his petite wife, Mona, arrived.

"We just came from church," Jackson said, "and didn't bring suits, so we'll just sit on the sidelines and watch the youngsters have fun."

"How about a cold one while they frolic," Dutton suggested. "A Heineken?"

Jackson nodded acceptance, his wife politely declining for now. "You have a lovely place," she said to Lydia Dutton.

"Let me show you around while the men talk business, which they always seem to be doing."

Relaxing under an expansive awning, Jackson got right to business. "You know we're playing with a couple of ticking bombs, Andy?"

"Couldn't agree more. That's why I wanted you to meet the people involved. I'll introduce you to them all when they get out of the water. You can see they're all spirited."

"And attractive," Jackson said. "Almost looks like Hollywood casting. I assume the statuesque woman in the string ensemble is the erstwhile honey pot?"

"You're right on that, Wayne. Can you believe that Dickerson didn't succumb to her enticements?"

"I've heard he's unusual. In any event, I want to make sure they all understand how delicate this operation is. I'll try to convey that message when we talk with them later. Now let's enjoy your beautiful surroundings, and do justice to the brewer's art."

"To everyone's health," Dutton toasted as they raised their beer cans.

The family dog, Rambo, a large black Lab, with a star-adorned red, white, and blue scarf around his neck, wandered around passively like he owned the place, moseying up to Jackson who patted him affectionately before he wandered off. "He's recovering from hip surgery," Dutton explained. "Getting old, and not as nimble as he was, but he's part of the family."

"Love dogs," Jackson said. "Loyal to the end."

Chapter Seventeen

"She's very attractive," Anna said to Del as they treaded water near the diving board.

"She was once a model," Del responded.

"How do you know?"

Del immediately visualized Nadia's photo album, and its nude poses. "She told me," he finally said.

"And you wrestle with her at Tae Kwon Do?"

"It's not wrestling, Anna. It's called martial arts, and includes a spiritual element."

"Hmm. Do you think she's beautiful?"

Del fluttered his arms to maintain buoyancy. "I believe some would say that. Isn't beauty said to be in the eyes of the beholder?"

"I asked if you thought she's beautiful?"

"Not as beautiful as you, Anna. Now can we get off that subject and just have fun?"

"For now," she said, paddling away.

* * *

"You look like a machine plowing through the water," Cynthia Chalmers told Kevin Ryan when he surfaced near her at the end of the pool.

"Used to do a lot of that," he said, addressing the well-formed woman in a snug red bikini.

"You were a SEAL, I understand."

"Seven years. Seven wet years. Mostly good years."

"Lots of memories, right?"

"Many good ones. Some not so."

"I know what you mean."

"You're ex-military too, right?"

"Air Force. Helo pilot."

"With many memories, I assume."

"Correct. Mixed, like yours."

"We need to compare notes sometime."

"Look forward to it sometime, but how about a race now? See how an Airedale matches up with a fish?"

"You're on," he said, watching her dive under the surface.

* * *

"I was supposed to be in church," Nadia was telling Curt Oswald as they sat on the edge of the pool at the shallow end, feet dangling in the undulating water.

"Dressed like that?" the former seminarian said with a laugh.

Nadia's eyes scanned the skimpy black fabric. "A little too little? There's often less in Europe. Sometimes nothing."

Oswald nodded. "That's what I've heard."

"Guess I need to become more Americanized, Curt. I hope I haven't offended anyone. I'm depending on you and Cynthia for protection."

"You can bet on that, and I don't consider myself a prude. You look fine to me."

"Thanks. I don't want there to be any secrets between us."

Oswald grinned. "Don't see how."

"Oh, the American sense of humor surfaces again," Nadia said, elbowing Oswald. "I heard that you studied to be a priest. What changed your plans?"

"The staff running the seminary finally concluded I wasn't fit for a life of chastity. I agreed, and we parted on friendly terms."

"So you went from one monastery to another?"

"Seems like it at times. Discipline and such—quite similar in many respects."

"But no vow of chastity, right?"

"Right."

"My church allows married clergy. In fact, the pastor I was supposed to listen to today has three children."

"They had married priests in mine in past centuries."

Nadia smiled. "How did we turn from my near nudity to religion?"

"Divine providence perhaps," Oswald said, elbowing her back. "We studied world religions in the seminary. I was always fascinated by Russian Orthodox rituals."

"You'll have to join me for one of our services."

"I'll put that high on my to-do list. Right now, I believe the others are signaling us to join them for a water polo game. Think you can stay within your suit with the exertion?"

"Let's find out, shall we?" Nadia said heading for the action.

* * *

With the energetic water exercise over, Nadia barely retaining her top, the participants were dressed and everyone assembled on the expansive poolside patio. Looming like silent sentries was a deluxe Weber grill and large corn steamer.

"Help yourselves to drinks," Dutton announced. "Beer, water, and soft drinks are in the coolers. Wine is on the bar, along with the harder stuff if desired. Then I'll introduce our special guest."

With beverages selected, everyone's eyes focused on Assistant Director Wayne Jackson.

But, before Jackson could speak, loud, frantic barking echoed from the deep end of the pool. All heads turned. "Rambo!" Lydia Dutton shouted and the group rushed that way. "He's floundering!" Lydia screamed, seconds after a loud splash was heard and Del was in the water by the thrashing animal.

"Easy does it," he assured the dog as he cradled the panicked pet in his arms. "You're okay, pal" he soothed, moving him to the side of the pool where helping hands lifted him onto the pool apron. Sight of the dog's patriotic scarf prompted him to begin whistling *Yankee Doodle Dandy*.

While Dutton and his wife administered to their prized pet, Anna snuggled against her dripping fiancée. "My hero," she murmured.

"Well done," Ryan said as the others voiced similar congratulations.

"Thanks," Dutton said. "I'll get you some dry clothes."

Five minutes later, with Del dressed in one of Dutton's jumpsuits and Rambo resting contentedly at Del's feet, Dutton resumed his introduction.

"Most of you have heard of the legendary Wayne Jackson, and some have met him," Dutton began. "He was an All-American tight end at Syracuse University where he set all kinds of records before he blew a knee in Steelers rookie camp and decided to join the Bureau. He's continued his record of success in the FBI, managing many of our most complex cases. He's accompanied by his lovely wife, Mona."

"My secret weapon," Jackson interjected. "Keeps me focused."

"The Assistant Director has a message for all of us," Dutton said, "so I'll ask him to take over."

With a dazzling smile displaying brilliant white teeth, contrasting with his smooth mahogany complexion, Jackson opened light heartedly. "After that display of excellence my words might sound trite, but I'll do what my mama told me long ago. She said when I was making a speech to stand up, speak up, and shut up quickly, so this will be brief. The Director is personally following your cases, and sends his regards. I'll be briefing him on what occurred at this white supremacy meeting. Well, maybe not everything," he said with a broad smile. "Suffice it to say, what you're undertaking is critically important to the security of our country, and these cases are of the highest priority. Sounds sort of corny, but true. We recognize the danger you are placing yourselves in, especially the ladies, and assure you of our complete support. You must rely on each other to make the operation successful. At the same time you must maintain total confidentiality. No discussing your activities with anyone outside this group. We're already dealing with one leak, which I'm happy to report has been plugged, but we can't afford another. Remember, lives are at stake. Are there any questions?"

Kevin Ryan asked if headquarters had set any timetable for concluding the cases.

"Immediately, if not sooner," Jackson answered to general laughter. "Seriously, that's our goal."

Nadia raised her hand. "Will my grandparents be able to join me in freedom?"

"Absolutely," Jackson assured. "Things are already in motion, though I can't go into details."

"I'm trusting you with our lives," Nadia said.

"And that trust won't be broken, Ms. Rostov," Jackson said with certitude.

Jackson looked around. "Any other questions?"

With no apparent queries forthcoming, Del spoke up. "When do we eat?"

Amidst the laughter, Rambo licked his caressing hand.

* * *

"I warned you he was different," Dutton said good naturedly to Jackson fifteen minutes later as the big grill was heating up.

"But he brought in a valuable defector," Jackson noted, watching his wife helping Lydia Dutton set an oversize picnic table. "And he likes dogs."

"Yes, that's the paradox. Along with that, he's got some mysterious appeal to women. You see how his fiancée and Nadia tend to hover over him? Maybe it's the mothering instinct."

"Whatever works, Andy. Keep him healthy, and speaking of healthy, that meat doesn't look like hamburger to me."

"Special occasion, Wayne. Giant had a sale on New York strips. I'm buttering up my boss."

"You know you don't need to do that. I'd be the first to endorse your advancement."

"Didn't we just have that discussion? I'm happy where I am."

Jackson scanned the surroundings.

"I've been very fortunate, Wayne. Lydia inherited the house and our large lot—acre and a half—before property became so expensive. Gives us lots of privacy. We hardly ever see or hear our neighbors. There's a retired doctor to my right, and a world-traveling college professor next to him who I hear rented out his place. Lots of seclusion only a few miles from the boiling cauldron of Washington. In short, I like it here."

Jackson nodded understanding. "I can see why. Pretty fancy, steaks and all."

"Simple Americana, Wayne. You also get corn on the cob and my wife's super salad. In addition, though we told our folks not to bring anything, Cynthia Chalmers arrived with a chocolate layer cake; Anna brought a bottle of Chinese plum wine; and Nadia presented a fifth of Russian vodka."

"Oh for the simple life," Jackson chortled. "My bottle of Drambuie for after dinner is in the car."

"Hey, Wayne. This respite ends tomorrow. Let's enjoy today."

"I'll drink to that," Jackson said, opening his second Heineken.

* * *

Dutton invited Oswald to say the grace as the group gathered around the table. "He's had a lot of practice, I understand."

The former seminarian delivered a succinct non-denominational message, imploring Divine guidance, thanks for everyone's blessings and the bounteous food, appreciation for America's gifts, and success in the group's endeavors.

"Nicely done," Nadia murmured from her seat at his side.

"Maybe you could do a closing grace in Russian," he suggested.

"Sure," she said, grabbing an ear of corn. "I've always had trouble eating these."

"Just chomp your pretty teeth on the cob and start chewing. It comes naturally."

"You're fun when you relax," she said.

"It's enjoyable relaxing with you," Oswald said, spearing a steaming steak from the passing platter.

"I think I'm going to enjoy this assignment," Nadia concluded.

* * *

Dinner conversation was light with humorous banter. The rich dessert prompted cheers and groans. Jackson retrieved the Drambuie from his car and toasted the group with assurances of total success. "We need to do this more often," he said. "It symbolizes the historic FBI family culture."

"We'll have the reunion here when this all goes down," Dutton pledged.

Nadia fulfilled her offer with a short blessing in Russian. "It essentially says 'God be with us'," she explained.

As the gathering began to dissolve, Del and Anna said they were headed for their new quarters in the Westin Hotel.

Cynthia volunteered to ride home with Kevin Ryan, since "he is all by himself."

Oswald lowered his convertible top for the trip home, "It might be a little chilly," he cautioned Nadia.

"Not for a warm-blooded Russian woman," she assured.

Jackson and Dutton viewed the departures, holding glasses of Drambuie on the rocks. "Mona is driving," Jackson declared. "Don't need a public embarrassment. Two Jack Daniels were J. Edgar's limit, I've been told by the old timers. Seemed to work for him. So here's to our rich history," he toasted.

Del and Anna stopped to say goodnight, the newly nicknamed "hero of the pool" redressed in jeans and sport shirt. "Thanks, sir, for reinforcing my confidence in the FBI family."

Dutton patted his charge on the shoulder. "We're indebted to you, but," he said with assumed sternness, "don't you dare try to steal the affections of our dog!"

Del grinned. "Wouldn't think of it, boss. He knows where he has a cool pool," he said, again whistling a few bars of *Yankee Doodle Dandy,* which prompted the dog's tail to thump rhythmically.

Dutton chuckled. "Has anyone figured you out?"

"Anna's getting close. Thanks for a great day."

"Truly one of a kind," Dutton murmured to his huddling wife as they waved goodbye. Rambo barked farewell. "Heaven help us," Dutton said as they watched the disappearing taillights of the last departing guests. "It's going to be 24/7 from now on with this cast of characters."

Lydia Dutton laughed lightly. "And you also seem to be supervising a dating service. Good luck."

Chapter Eighteen

"This isn't as large as the Ritz-Carlton suite, but it's very nice," Anna said as she surveyed Del's Westin Hotel room.

"I'm sure the Bureau will spring for a separate room for you if you wish," Del said. "We don't know how long this inquiry into Congressman Walters might last."

"This is fine with me," Anna assured, bouncing on the King-sized bed.

"Will Mrs. Fong be upset about your extended absence from work?"

"No, she said to take all the time I needed, 'as long as that young man behaves himself.'"

Del laughed. "She's always threatening a tong war. Assure her I'm the essence of fidelity."

"You better be, or I might be tempted to explore some of the 'comforting' Walters suggested."

"That pig. Still think I should have served him a knuckle sandwich."

"Save it until really needed, my hero. Now we better get some sleep in preparation for my call to him tomorrow."

"Sleep?" Del inquired.

"Eventually," she said, turning down the gold bedspread. Her breath momentarily halted and her eyes drilled Del's. "What are those red marks on the pillow?"

* * *

"You travel in style," Cynthia Chalmers told Kevin Ryan as they flowed through light Sunday evening traffic in Ryan's red Corvette.

"Boy toy," Ryan replied. "Provides a surge of pleasure when I get enough time to indulge."

"Not my business, perhaps, and pardon my candor, but you're what a lot of women would call a choice specimen."

Ryan chuckled. "Thanks for the accolade. I won't say there have not been opportunities, but, in the spirit of full disclosure, I was on the brink of matrimony prior to an extended SEAL deployment. When I returned, I was politely informed that my would-be bride, Jessica, had concluded that she couldn't handle the uncertainty of my job. I give her credit for her honesty. We parted as friends. She married a stable dentist, has two kids in their comfortable suburban home. I hope she's happy. Since then, I guess I've been pretty much married to my Bureau job."

"Thanks for the confidence, Kevin. I think Jessica missed out on a good guy."

"Kind of you to say. Do you have a true confession story as well?"

Cynthia laughed. "Seems like I just talked about this with Oswald, after years of trying to forget. Have you been talking with him?"

"Not a word," Ryan said, changing his satellite radio channel to a golden oldies station.

Cynthia waited a beat. "Like you, I was almost left at the altar, only in my case it was in the form of an IED in Iraq that obliterated my co-pilot, who was also my fiancé."

"That's rough, Cynthia. Those cowardly attacks really piss me off."

"Yeah, you might expect getting hit in the air, but we were in a motor convoy on a dusty goat path they call roads."

"A lot of animals over there, Cynthia, which encourages me to work night and day to keep them out of our country."

"Amen, we share those goals. It's good to talk with someone who understands."

"We should do it again. By the way, you told me you live in Falls Church, but not the street."

"A townhouse on Kings Garden Way, near the Library, just off Leesburg Pike. I share it with a CIA Analyst. She works crazy hours too, so we rarely see each other."

"Got it," Ryan said. "That's close to me. I have a long-term rental at Fairfax Towers on Pimmit Drive. Our world is getting smaller. Nadia's apartment is just up the hill on Pimmit."

"And our office is only a mile or so from there," Cynthia said. "In addition, Anna and Del are temporarily at the Westin just inside the Beltway a few blocks away."

"There goes the neighborhood," Ryan joked, pulling up in front of Cynthia's residence.

"Thanks for the buggy ride, Kevin. It was fun."

"My pleasure. We need to pursue our common interests."

"I'm told I make a good meatloaf."

"One of my favorites. Sleep well. See you in the office."

* * *

"Sure you're not too cold?" Oswald asked Nadia.

"No, I'm used to it. It feels a lot like Moscow weather. Your heater keeps my feet warm, and the rest of my body enjoys the stimulation."

"Good thing you changed out of your, ah, bathing suit."

"Still thinking about that, are you?"

"Hard not to. You filled it out well."

Nadia paused. "You know my background. Exposure was sometimes a way of life."

"And survival, Nadia. I'm aware of what your country demanded of you. You didn't have a whole lot of choice."

"Thanks. You don't condemn me then?"

"That's not my role, and I've said before that forgiveness is a big part of my belief that what's in the past belongs there. It's the present, and future, that counts."

"You make me feel cleansed, Curt. Thanks. Funny how our conversation always seems to end up with skin and sin."

"And redemption," he added. "Better days ahead is one of my favorite slogans."

Nadia leaned over and delivered a moist kiss as he pulled up in front of her apartment. "I'd invite you up, but I don't want to lose this holy glow."

Oswald returned a similarly hearty kiss. "Your wisdom matches your beauty. Better safe than sorry."

"Tell whoever selected you to help protect my body that they made a good choice."

"I'm sure it will be a pleasure, Nadia."

"Well stated," she said leaving the car.

Chapter Nineteen

"Well!" Anna demanded, moving her eyes between Del and the red smear.

"Beats me," Del said. "It's not mine."

"I'm glad to hear that. But whom then? It's the shade a brunet would wear. Anyone come to mind?"

Del pondered. "Nadia?"

"I had that thought too."

"But she's never been here. Might be the maids."

"On your pillow?"

"That's not my pillow."

"It's a pillow on your bed!"

"Anna, let's not argue. I have no idea where it came from."

Anna sniffled. "I'm sorry, Del. I'm not accusing you of anything. Guess I just feel a bit threatened by the gorgeous woman you wrestle with."

"We don't wrestle, I told you, and you have no cause to feel threatened by her or anyone else. I love you, and am fully committed to us." He paused and scratched his head. "Hmm, I gave my room key to Kevin the other day. He said Cynthia needed it."

"Cynthia! She's good looking too!"

Del raised his hands in a surrender gesture. "Honey, there are three other pillows with no lipstick stains on them. Let's use them and get some sleep."

"Cynthia?" Anna muttered, heading for the bathroom.

* * *

TYSONS CORNER

"You look worried," Ryan told Del when they arrived at the office about the same time Monday morning.

"Anna's upset about some lipstick smear on a pillow in my room at the Westin. She hints that I had a woman there—possibly Nadia. I remember you said that Cynthia needed to use my key,"

Ryan put a comforting hand on Del's shoulder. "Relax. Cynthia met with Nadia there, along with Curt. I'm sure it wasn't Curt's. Probably belonged to either Nadia or Cynthia."

"I'm innocent. I wasn't there," Del proclaimed.

Ryan grinned. "The problem's solved. I'll tell Anna."

"Boy, it doesn't take much to cause a problem, does it?"

"It's the little things that can throw you off the track, Del. Now let's get to our meeting and stay on the track."

Thirty minutes later, with Anna pacified, Del's normally bubbly outlook restored, and the relaxed weekend a happy memory, the participants pursued their assigned tasks with renewed vigor. During their conference room session they discussed a unit name, eventually agreeing they would adopt the nickname "Trappers."

"Sounds fitting," Dutton said. "Anna will be calling Congressman Walters this morning, and Nadia meets with Alexei Markov this afternoon. We have the necessary tech and surveillance support arranged. Good luck, Trappers."

* * *

WASHINGTON, D.C.

"Well, what a nice way to start the week," U.S. Congressman Jason Walters said in his mellifluous voice when his administrative aide patched through the call from Ms. Anna Chen. "I've been thinking of how striking you looked at the reception the other night, and apologize if I offended you by bringing up old memories."

"Thank you. I must admit being startled with the recollections."

"Understandable, Anna. You undoubtedly have some painful memories."

"That's what I'm calling you about, Jason. You made reference to some past activities that involved the Chairman and me. It's bothered me since our conversation."

"I hate to see such a lovely lady bothered. As I told you, I feel obligated to offer comfort to those I respect."

"A noble trait, Jason."

"It brings me satisfaction to help old friends, like you. Why don't we get together personally to discuss things? Much better than on the phone. You said you now live in California. How much longer will you be in D.C.?"

"A few more days."

"Well then, how about dinner, say tomorrow night?"

"I believe that will fit in with my schedule, Jason."

"Good. How about The Four Seasons on Pennsylvania Avenue—say seven?"

"Yes, that would be fine. It was one of the favorite places the Chairman and I frequented."

* * *

Anna shuddered when she hung up. "I feel soiled when I talk to that man."

Ryan, who had monitored her call, nodded. "Sure you can carry this out?"

Anna sat back in her chair. "No question, Kevin. It's distasteful, but I'm fully in. Don't worry. I won't let the Trappers down."

"I'm sure of that, Anna. And I'm optimistic that Walters will hang himself during your contacts. The authorized tap worked fine. Visualize trapping a rodent."

BURKE LAKE PARK

Curt Oswald and Cynthia Chalmers were again monitoring the meet of Nadia and Alexei from an unobtrusive surveillance van. Sounds from Nadia's concealed mic came across on their recording equipment clearly.

"You can hear her breathe," Chalmers observed.

"And I'm getting good videos of her familiar friend who just walked up," Oswald said.

"Where were you Sunday?" Alexei demanded with his opening words.

Nadia paused briefly before responding, her heart pounding. *He must know I wasn't in church.* "I was sick in bed," she finally responded.

"You said you were going to church."

"That's right. I planned to, but ate something Saturday night that did me in. And, how did you know I wasn't in church? Are you spying on me?"

"Sophia Petrov from the Embassy Annex attends that church. She said she didn't see you."

"So you are spying on me! I resent that!"

"We need to know who is loyal, Nadia. You know what happens if someone betrays us."

"I'm well aware, Alexei. Why should I trust you?"

"Because I'm your handler, and responsible for you."

"Well, if you expect me to get the information you want, you better handle me with more respect."

"I'd like to handle you," Alexei said in a suggestive tone.

"Cold day, Alexei."

"We'll see. Now, what have you learned? I can't keep our superiors happy much longer."

Nadia passed him an envelope. "Here's what I learned from translating at the meeting the space techs had at the Embassy last week. It's brief, but apparently critical. It's all in my report. Hopefully, there will be more at their next meeting this week."

"I'll pass it along, but keep trying. Are you still doing the martial arts with that FBI agent?"

"Yes, I'm supposed to attend a session tomorrow."

"And you don't think he's on to you?"

"No indications. Like I told you, he seems a little dense."

"They don't usually hire dumbbells."

"This time I think they did."

"Okay, Nadia. I need to go, in case someone is watching."

"Like you're watching me, Alexei? That bothers me."

"Part of the trade. I'd like to watch you in action."

"Khui," (Prick) Nadia said in departing.

* * *

"She gave it to the guy with gusto," Cynthia commented with admiration.

Oswald chuckled. "I'm sure Del will be thrilled to hear her comments about him."

Chapter Twenty

WASHINGTON, D.C.

Del drove Anna to the steps of the Lincoln Memorial where she hailed a cab. "In case he sees you arrive at the Four Seasons," he explained.

They had spent the afternoon rehearsing her role and planning how to explore Walters' involvement in criminal acts.

The question of entrapment was debated with the office's legal advisor. "He's the one who brought it up," the advisor concluded. "I believe we're okay."

Cynthia helped Anna get comfortable with a mic concealed under her skirt. "I'm becoming an expert on this," she remarked. "Think I'll add it to my resume."

The maître d' at the dining room flashed a sign of recognition as Anna approached his station. "Good evening Ms. Chen. It's been a long time since we've been honored with your presence. Welcome back."

"Thank you, Henri. You are looking well."

"As are you."

"I'm supposed to meet Congressman Walters. Has he arrived yet?" Anna inquired.

The headwaiter maintained a stoic expression that Anna thought contained a hint of disapproval. "Yes, he's here. Let me lead you to his table."

"Anna! So nice of you to come," Walters greeted while he placed a martini glass on his table and struggled to his feet.

"Good evening, Jason, thank you for the invitation."

"My pleasure. I don't like to dine or drink alone. I'm having a Bombay gin martini. What would you like?"

"White wine would be fine," Anna replied, taking her seat.

"It rhymes," Walters said with a laugh. "White wine, fine. A far-east talent perhaps?"

"Perhaps."

"You brought many talents from your homeland, your old associate told me. We talked frequently and he highly praised you."

A hovering waiter recommended a chardonnay and took Anna's order as she debated a response. "I wasn't aware you were that close to the Chairman," she finally said.

"Oh, we were," Walters assured in a boastful tone, "but not openly, except for occasional golf rounds. We thought it best to keep our business dealings private."

"Is that why I didn't see your name mentioned in that commodities legislation prosecution?"

Walters frowned. "Persecution is a better word. Those eager-beaver FBI hounds hurt a lot of my friends."

"But not you?"

Walters smirked. "They didn't even interview me. They apparently knew I wasn't involved in that legislation."

"You are obviously a careful and clever man."

Walters emitted a self- satisfying smile while he signaled the waiter. "A Bombay refill, Roger, and another for the lady whenever she's ready."

"I'm fine, thank you."

"Indeed," Walters said with a leer. "Quite fine. I've taken the liberty of ordering Chateaubriand for us. Does that meet with your pleasure?"

"That's fine, Jason."

"It's juicy, Anna. I want to insure your pleasure."

"You mentioned juicy details about me and the Chairman. Would you like to elaborate?"

Walters raised his fresh martini. "Eventually, but let's first enjoy each other's company. Tell me what you've been doing since the untimely death of the Chairman."

Anna sighed internally as she visualized facing a ravenous beast. "I had a lengthy recovery from my injuries in the accident," Anna began. "Then I traveled home to Taiwan to see my mother who was seriously ill, eventually returning to San Francisco after her recovery. I currently live and work there." Anna made no mention of her heavy involvement in major FBI cases.

"And that young man you were with at the reception?"

"He's my fiancé. His name is Del."

"What does he do?"

"He sells insurance."

"Doesn't sound exciting for a spirited woman like you."

"He's comfortable," Anna said.

"But a bit dull?"

Anna nodded. "He doesn't exude the prestige or electricity of someone like you."

"My position does carry weight," Walters agreed, draining his glass. "I always admired your ambition, Anna. You've gone through a lot, and deserve a richer life."

Anna sipped from her glass before responding. "And what might that be?"

Walters leaned closer. "Some of the business arrangements the Chairman and I shared are still in operation. I'm sure he would have liked his intimate friend to enjoy some of their benefits."

Anna's look was questioning. "He didn't discuss many of his business dealings with me, but I gathered from overhearing some of his conversations that there were risks involved. I need to ask, therefore, if they were completely legal."

Walters released a half smile. "I like your candor. Verifies my belief in your grit."

"I'm a legal immigrant, Jason, and I don't want to jeopardize my status by doing something unlawful."

"Good thinking, Anna. I'm likewise adverse to tangling with the law, but I believe one of our extracurricular projects meets legal requirements, and offers nice profit potential."

"If you are so confident of its success, why do you wish to share it with me?"

Walters leaned back and removed his glasses. "I'm a man who appreciates beauty and gets lonely at times. I can afford a high standard of living that relishes pleasant companionships. I like excitement."

"Aren't you married?"

"Not in Washington."

"But you have a wife in New Jersey?"

"True, but that's beside the point. The Chairman had a wife too."

Anna's face flushed. "I know."

Walters took another drink from his glass. "Let's not dwell on the past. There's an opportunity now to make some money that will improve our lives. A smart woman like you could help me close a deal on the business matter I referred to."

Their discussion was interrupted by the arrival of their meal, and they watched as their veteran waiter served the dishes and carved the steaming beef. They concentrated on the succulent feast and engaged in casual discussion about weather and international news. A bottle of California merlot was mainly consumed by Walters, and they finished the meal with a chocolate parfait dessert.

"Now you have to admit this is living in style," Walters declared, emptying his wine glass. "We can make this a regular thing."

"It was delicious, Jason, I'll need to walk miles tomorrow to work it off."

"Don't overdo it. You look in perfect form to me. Think about our discussion and we can talk further."

"It's a lot to think about. You only talked in general terms. You weren't very specific."

"True, Anna. I just wanted to explore your willingness to do something exciting, make some money, and have some fun along the way. By way of a hint, it's related to the insurance industry and its many forthcoming changes. In my legislative position I am privy to knowledge that could prove highly profitable."

"It does sound enticing, Jason."

"I guarantee it," he said, "but I need some indication of your possible participation. You might have to delay your return to San Francisco."

"I'll sleep on it, Jason, and thanks for the elegant dinner. It brought back memories of such events in the past."

"How will you get home?" he asked.

"I'll take a cab to my hotel."

"You never mentioned where you were staying."

"The Westin in Tysons Corner."

"With the insurance salesman?"

Anna nodded.

"We should upgrade you from that arrangement," Walters muttered. "Call me at my apartment at the Watergate." He handed her another business card with his personal cell number written on the back.

They walked out together, Walters a little wobbly on his feet. The maître d' bid them both farewell, subtly conveying another hint of disapproval. A doorman quickly had them seated in separate cabs that swiftly whisked them away.

Oh, Del, I can't wait to feel your loving arms around me, was Anna's thought as her cab headed for the Key Bridge.

Chapter Twenty-one

TYSONS CORNER

"You did great," Kevin Ryan complimented as Anna was debriefed the morning after her dinner meeting with Congressman Walters.

"I felt like a basket case when I got back to Del. He brought me back to life."

"She really looked shook," Del concurred.

"I again ask if this is too hard on you, Anna?"

"No, Kevin. I'm more determined than ever now. He's not a nice man."

"That's for certain," said Andy Dutton who had just walked in. "I listened to the tape. It looks like he has his grubby hands on upcoming health care legislation. However he slipped through the net on the SHARKS commodities scheme, it appears we can finally nab him on the health care insurance deal. Smells like a bribery plot."

"Possibly involving some lobbyists," Ryan commented.

"They're everywhere," Dutton said. "A generally respected profession, but with more than enough shady characters to give them all an unsavory reputation. We need to find out just what his deal is, and whom it involves. The corrupt farm commodities plotters are still in prison, aren't they?"

Ryan nodded. "Last we checked. Doubt it could be any of them."

"The mic worked well," Dutton said, directing a look at Chalmers. "Good work, Cynthia. Are we ready to push forward on the next round?" he asked the group.

The heads of all the Trappers nodded assent.

"Okay," Dutton said to Anna. "Call the louse."

***

ANNANDALE, VA

Nadia arrived at the Tae Kwon Do studio a few minutes before Del, who quickly positioned himself next to her with the dozen or so other adults assembled for limbering up exercises. Between a series of kicks and hand thrusts shouted by the Master, they managed to exchange a few words.

"I'm being watched," Nadia said.

"Here?" Del grunted.

"No, but possibly outside," Nadia said between exercises. "They knew I wasn't in church Sunday."

"You were followed to Dutton's?" Del questioned with alarm.

"I don't think so, but it appears they're checking out all their 'helpers.'"

"We'll have to tighten our counter-intelligence coverage," Dell said as they paired up for one-on-one sparring. "We need to be particularly careful of who you're seen with, and where. They don't know Cynthia and Curt as people in your life, so they have to be our lifeline," Del huffed, moving out of Nadia's reach.

"Don't I still have you?" Nadia asked.

"I'm always at your service," Del said, spinning away.

"Almost, anyway," Nadia replied, stepping in deftly and delivering a sharp jab in Del's ribs. "Don't forget me."

Del felt relieved when the session ended and they walked out together, pausing near their parked cars.

"If there are watchers checking tonight, they think I'm trying to seduce you," Nadia said. "Make it look authentic," she added, opening her arms.

Del felt duty-bound to comply, responding with a spirited embrace and lingering kiss.

"Nice," Nadia said, concluding the embrace with a pinch of his buttocks. "Hope it doesn't leave a bruise," she said with a smile. "Your lovely lady might not understand."

"Ah, Nadia. Give a guy a break," Del implored.

"Tell Anna how lucky she is," Nadia said, unlocking her door.

* * *

Nadia's spirits were elevated when she checked her cell phone and found a missed call from Curt Oswald. He wondered if they might be able to meet for a drink at the Lido restaurant on Leesburg Pike at eight. She glanced at her dashboard clock. Just enough time, she estimated. Might be fun to further our interests in religion and such.

FALLS CHURCH, VA

Oswald was seated at a small table in a back corner of the softly lit Italian cafe, back to the wall, with a clear view of the entrance door.

Nadia immediately spotted him and joined him at his table.

"I was hoping you could make it," he said, rising to welcome her.

"I didn't take the time to reply," she said. "I knew a disciplined man like you would be where he said he would be."

"Discipline has its limitations, Nadia, but I was banking on you."

"So, here I am," she said brightly. "What will we discuss tonight, sin or redemption?"

"Both if you wish, but I'd like to get to know more about an intriguing lady. Might I loosen her tongue with a glass of whatever?"

Nadia smiled. "It won't be my native drink, Curt. I've learned how devilish it can render a person."

"There's that old devil creeping back into the conversation again," he laughed. "So what's your pleasure tonight?"

"A glass of chardonnay sounds safe. But before I reveal my checkered past, tell me a little about yourself."

"Before I subject you to that boring subject, are you hungry? Their pizza and lasagna are wonderful. I just finished with the house special."

"Thanks, but I had a large lunch. I'll just munch on the bread sticks and sip away."

A young waitress arrived to take Nadia's drink order, and Curt requested a refill of Chianti before he began a background summary.

"I was born in Detroit to a middle class family of Irish-German heritage. Two wonderful sisters. My dad was an electrical contractor with enough income to afford sending me to an all-boys Catholic High School where I was mediocre in several sports but well educated by a dedicated religious staff that excelled in discipline. The good Fathers there thought I had potential for the religious life and the seminary followed for five years until the lack of a strong vocation became apparent and I was cast free. A friend recommended I check out the Bureau, which I did and found a comfortable fit. After graduation from the Academy at Quantico, I served three years in Omaha and was then transferred here. End of story."

Nadia smiled. "You didn't mention women in your life."

Oswald smiled back. "No, I didn't. There were a few of them, but to answer an unasked question, I happen to like women. Sometimes too much, perhaps."

"Thanks, Curt. I didn't mean to invade your privacy, but it's good to know where a person stands. I see you as a decent young man who, I suspect, has been told by a number of ladies that he's pretty good looking too."

Oswald flushed. "You have a kind and flattering manner. I can see why you have been successful."

"'In my 'dubious profession' you didn't add."

"I understand the circumstances you faced, Nadia."

"It was contrary to everything my religion taught. It isn't easy to survive in a Godless society."

"But you have, and you're free, and have a full life of happiness before you."

"You provide such encouragement, Curt. It will be complete when I'm reunited with my grandparents in your wonderful country."

"And that will happen. Now, educate me about your upbringing."

Nadia recounted her early years and comfortable life before being recruited by government agents. "They were looking for certain types."

"Like healthy, beautiful and intelligent young women."

She nodded. "With the added appeal of serving their country. They made it sound very patriotic, plus the added incentive of it being advantageous to their families."

"With strong hints that anything less than wholehearted effort could be detrimental to the health and welfare of you and your family, right?"

"Yes, that was made abundantly clear in our 'academy.' It was a far cry from your training institution."

"I've read studies of what occurred there. Rather shocking."

"I don't know what you've read, but it's probably true. They were quite thorough in their instructions, employing some of their more successful 'graduates' to train new recruits."

"While I don't want to subject you to reliving unpleasant experiences, it might help us in confronting future infiltration attempts if you gave us a summary of your training. Could you do that?"

"Why not? It might be therapeutic, and possibly educational for any of your agents who might be so engaged."

Oswald shook his head. "We don't do that."

"You have female agents, don't you?"

"Of course. About a quarter or so of our complement. Cynthia's a good example."

"She's very attractive. I'm sure that has helped her solve cases."

"Yes, but she and our other female agents have done great work without compromising personal integrity."

"I hear what you're saying, but aren't they sometimes in, ah, challenging situations where their femininity might be an advantage?"

"Yeah, I can imagine that," Oswald said, recalling hearing about a female agent working undercover as an Atlantic City chorus girl to penetrate the SHARKS fraud conspiracy. "But there are rules and guidelines regarding how far they can go."

"I'm sure there are, and I don't suggest that they employ Russian methods."

"The Bureau expects all of their employees to abide by a proper moral code."

Nadia sipped from her glass. "The spy game can get dicey at times. Fine lines might sometimes get crossed."

Oswald looked thoughtful. "You display your sagacity, Nadia. The real world can be confusing, can't it?"

"Not everything is black and white," she said, picking up her glass of white wine.

Oswald raised his glass of Chianti and touched it against hers. "To a harmonious blend," he toasted.

She drained her glass. "I'm glad you're one of my bodyguards. Will you guard my route home?"

Chapter Twenty-two

FALLS CHURCH, VA

"Interesting," the man behind the wheel of a black Honda said from his position across the street from Nadia's apartment.

"Yes, very interesting, Alexei," his companion agreed, watching the headlights of the Buick convertible blink as the car it appeared to be escorting turned into the apartment parking area. "Does Nadia have a new friend?"

"I couldn't see who was driving, Colonel, but it's worth checking out. Did you catch the license number?"

"Virginia JWJ something. I couldn't see the numbers. Be on the alert for that car in the future. We don't want our little treasure to fall into the wrong hands."

"Or arms," Alexei quipped.

"Yes," the portly older man replied with a snicker. "She belongs in the protective arms of her countrymen."

"Good luck. Nadia guards her treasure like a bank vault. She shut me off like a faucet."

"Maybe she would show more respect for a SVR Colonel. After all, she's my responsibility in that embassy matter. Perhaps I should afford her some personal attention."

"That might work, sir, but I didn't think we used military rank in our current assignments."

"You're absolutely right, Major, so tonight we're just Serge and Alexei, right?"

"By all means, sir, and I remain at your service."

"You are doing well, Alexei, and I see a bright future for you. It was good of you to arrange for me to see one of our honey pots in person. She is indeed a prize specimen. I've enjoyed our on-the-scene look."

"Maybe you'd enjoy more than a look, Colonel?"

"Serge, remember?"

"Oh, yes. My error."

"I'll let you correct that slight oversight, Alexei, by arranging a meeting for me with Ms. Rostov. I believe she might be in need of some personal guidance."

"I'll see what I can do, sir."

The senior officer directed a cold stare. "That was not a vague request, Major. Do it!"

Alexei gulped. "Yes, Colonel."

TYSONS CORNER

Kevin Ryan was just finishing his second cup of morning coffee when the call arrived from Nadia's secure cell phone. "A nice way to start the day," he said.

"It was for me, too, until I received an unexpected call this morning from Alexei. He wants a personal meeting ASAP. It wasn't scheduled."

"Where?"

"The parking lot of the West Falls Church Metro station. He wouldn't say why."

"What time?"

"Eleven a.m."

"Hmm. Plenty of time to launch Donny."

"Donny?"

"Our newest drone. He's an improved experimental guy."

"Or gal?"

Ryan laughed. "Gender to be determined. Cynthia is on her way to wire you up. Let's find out what it's all about."

* * *

FALLS CHURCH, VA

"I came in under guise of a house cleaner," Cynthia said as she entered Nadia's apartment.

"You don't look like a house cleaner," Nadia told the well-dressed woman.

"Curt would look less likely," Cynthia observed.

Nadia nodded. "You're right, and the placement of my recording equipment might embarrass him."

"He is a bit of a Boy Scout," Cynthia agreed.

"But boys will be boys, won't they?" Nadia said, lifting her skirt.

* * *

Nadia was parked in a remote corner of the almost full lot when Alexei approached on foot and slipped into her passenger seat. "What's going on?" she immediately questioned. "Why didn't you tell me on the phone? I had to call in sick at work."

Alexei put his left fingertips to his ear. "Never know who's listening."

"Aren't you getting paranoid?"

"Can't be too careful. An important person in your life is involved, and need not be distressed."

"And who might that be?"

"My superior, Colonel Serge Volkov."

"I've heard of him. I thought he was a Cultural Attaché at the Embassy."

Alexei looked indulgent. "You might look good, but not too bright in the head. He's SVR, with extensive experience in the old KGB. He worked with President Putin."

"Guess I shouldn't be surprised. And how is he involved in my life?"

"He's responsible for delivering the information you're too slow in gathering. His patience is running short."

"I'm doing the best I can. What more can I do?"

"Explain it to him. He wants to see you personally."

Nadia paused, contemplating possibilities. "Where? I doubt he wants me calling on him at the Russian Embassy."

"Of course not. It must be a public place. He lives well. *Morton's* on Connecticut Avenue at seven tomorrow night."

She nodded. "How will I recognize him?"

"Just ask for Mr. Winters."

"Winters?"

"Yeah, like winters in Moscow. Remember them?"

"Never forget them."

"Maybe you should take a trip home to refresh your memory. That could happen, you know, depending on how well you perform your current assignment."

"Are you threatening me, Alexei?"

The man responded with a semi-smirk. "How would someone loyal to their homeland consider that a threat? Be on time," he added. "And, before I forget it, do you know anyone who drives a white Buick convertible?"

TYSONS CORNER, VA

Cynthia Chalmers was reporting to Kevin Ryan on Nadia's meeting with her Russian handler. "It appears we have a new player, Kevin. Is his name familiar to you?"

"Oh, indeed. We've been long aware of his intelligence role under the cover of Cultural Attaché. Typical practice. This gives us another subject involved in the South Korean Embassy leaks. 'Donny' worked fine, by the way, as well as Nadia's equipment."

"Nadia's solid, Kevin, but do you think we can risk putting her in the grasp of Volkov?"

"If she's game, but I don't think we can take a chance of wiring her up. We'll need other coverage."

Chalmers smiled. "Looks like the females are fighting on the front line."

"Well, you know how that is, Cynthia, but I assure you us rear-echelon males are impressed by the work of the gentler sex. What about the white Buick convertible question?"

"It was Curt. He followed her home after they met for a drink. He kept going, by the way."

"Smart. They make an interesting pair, but we need to be especially careful about public sightings. Presents a challenge: he's assigned to help her; she's under scrutiny by her watchers; our opponents don't know she's working for us. Enough to cause a royal headache."

"Tuck it in, Kevin. That's why they're paying you the big bucks."

"Haw!" Ryan laughed. "Just about enough for a dinner at *Morton's*. Tomorrow okay with you?"

"Female agents are always prepared to do their duty."

"Good to hear. I'll make our reservation."

FBI Code Name: SPYTRAP

Chapter twenty-three

WASHINGTON, D.C.

Anna met Congressman Walters at the legendary Watergate Hotel in the aptly named Foggy Bottom section of Washington. "Come to the *Top of the Gate* rooftop lounge," he directed during their phone conversation. Part of Watergate's restaurant facilities, its view was striking, Anna observed as she reached his table.

"It's wonderful to see you again," Walters enthused, rising to greet her. "I hope your presence means you have decided to join me in our venture."

"I came to discuss that with you."

"Hector!" he called out to a hovering waiter. "We need drinks."

The neatly dressed server responded immediately and took their orders, white wine for her, a Chivas Regal scotch refill for him.

"These are the kind of surroundings you belong in," he declared, waving an arm at the picturesque expanse that included the Kennedy Center, the Potomac River, the Key and Arlington Bridges, the Washington Monument, and much of the Washington skyline. "This is your element, Anna."

"It is impressive," she agreed.

"Right," Walters said. "We'll enjoy a celebratory drink here, then go down to a more discreet *Kingbird* dining room for serious business. I must add that you are looking particularly alluring tonight."

Anna shuddered internally. "Thank you," she said.

* * *

"Their voices are coming in loud and clear," Special Agent Joe Moretti told his partner, Harry Swanson, from their surveillance van parked outside the Watergate on Virginia Avenue.

"Yeah, and this is a refreshing change from the embassy lookout assignment, though a bit cramped. The pillows are comfortable, though."

"Part of the glamorous life of FBI agents," Moretti snickered.

"The good part is it's only temporary, and a lot of our colleagues have enjoyed, what do they call it, seasoning?"

"Well, I'm beginning to feel well seasoned."

"Patience, partner. The glamour will come in time. Meanwhile, let's listen to how a noble legislator tries to screw another citizen."

* * *

After an hour on the rooftop lounge, Anna and Walters were seated at a secluded table in a remote corner of the ground-floor *Kingbird* restaurant. "What I'm about to tell you is just between you and me, Anna. Are you ready to proceed in confidence?"

"I'm ready to listen to what you have to say, and how I might be involved."

Walters took another generous gulp of Chivas Regal before proceeding. "I told you that the late Chairman and I engaged in some business opportunities."

"Yes, but I thought all of them had been identified by the FBI."

"Most, but not all," Walters said with a self-congratulatory smile.

"Oh?"

"We partnered in an import business."

"I know about the gem imports," Anna said.

"This was different from that. We set it up as insurance. He was a clever businessman of tremendous talent."

"I well know. What did the business involve?"

Walters leaned closer. "Ivory imports."

"Legal?"

"Debatable, you might say," Walters said after a pause. "You've heard of the elephant tusk ivory trade?"

"Yes, the killing of disappearing elephants for their ivory tusks. Awful."

"Could be, but the damage has been done, and someone has to profit from it. Why not us?"

"How?"

"The profits from our endeavors were considerable, but the international community was enraged about the slaughter so we agreed to keep our activity discreetly hidden until the heat was off. We put the proceeds into a safe deposit box."

"You said the profits were considerable. How considerable?"

"About two million dollars."

"I'd say that is considerable, Jason."

"Indeed, and that's where you come in."

"Me? How?"

Walters smiled. "The funds are safe, but currently inaccessible. That's why I was so delighted to run into you. It reminded me of how to recover the money."

"And, that would be how?"

Walters took another drink from his glass. "Do you remember signing some bank cards with the Chairman?"

Anna paused in thought. "He had me sign a lot of documents with him."

"Could one of them have been a safe deposit box access card?"

"Possibly."

"More than possibly. I've seen the card. It's sitting in a Maryland bank. It has my signature, and yours. I have a key to the box. We need both signatures to liberate two million dollars."

"Whew, that's rather startling."

"We both profit, Anna. Pretty simple. Imagine it. You have a million dollars to use any way you wish."

"But is it legal? I don't want to go to jail."

"No, no. Not a chance. No one but us knows what's in the box. The bank could care less. All they want is the yearly fee, which I've been paying. It's fool proof."

"It does sound appealing," Anna said. "You said something about health insurance. How does that fit in?"

Walters sat back. "We're in Washington, my dear. Nothing's uncomplicated here. Everything has a connection."

"You're such a dynamic man, Jason. You have my curiosity raised."

"That's why I know we'll make a great team. You're smart and beautiful, and soon to be rich. I need my share of the money for a down payment on another major investment."

"Go on."

"There's pending legislation I'm interested in. It needs a couple of more sure votes to pass. I have a pair of congressional colleagues who might be inclined to see it my way for reasonable contributions to their re-election campaigns—a half-million each."

"But wouldn't that leave you with nothing?"

Walters sipped again from his glass. "Didn't I mention connected items?"

"Yes, but…"

"I like enterprising small companies. There's one I started that would profit handsomely if the health care legislation passes. This is an expensive town to live in, you know, and I like to live well."

"You appear to do so," Anna said, gazing around the richly appointed dining room.

"And I have a comfortable apartment here, Anna, which I'm anxious to show you."

"That would be nice," she replied.

"Well, let's go then," Walters said with brightening eyes.

Anna looked at her watch. "Oh, I didn't realize it was so late. I need to get back to my hotel. Another time?"

Walters looked deflated. "To see the insurance salesman?"

Anna nodded.

"We have to do something about that complication."

Anna remained silent as Walters called for the check.

"So you'll help me gain access to the bank box?" he finally said.

"Hard to ignore an opportunity like that."

"Good, and next time we meet, don't plan on an early departure."

"Whatever you say, Jason."

You bet baby, was Walters thought as they parted.

In a pig's eye, Anna vowed to herself.

* * *

I hope that darkened van across the street heard all that, Anna thought as she left the Watergate and hailed a cruising cab.

In the van, Moretti summarized the conversation. "Getting interesting, Hank. The gal did well getting the guy talking about his deals."

"You could almost hear the good congressman panting about the chance of getting her in the sack."

"A million would be hard for most women to resist."

"Isn't she engaged to that Korean-speaking guy they brought in from California?"

"Yeah. Is that what you call a dilemma?"

Chapter Twenty-four

TYSONS CORNER

The group assembled in Kevin Ryan's office early the following morning had individually listened to the recorded conversation between Anna and Congressman Walters.

"Damn," Ryan said, "Anna elicited a ton of incriminating info. Give her my thanks and respect, Del."

"I will. She's sleeping in this morning. Pretty worn out from the session with Walters."

"A real congressional gem. No wonder the public holds them in such disrepute. A few rotten apples make them all look bad," Andy Dutton remarked. "But let's not get political. Let's see what we have."

"Sure sounds at least like intent to commit bribery," Ryan said.

"Yeah, we need to identify the two colleagues he referred to," Dutton reminded. "Lots of work to do."

Del had a question. "How do we proceed on the safe deposit box?"

"Simple. Have Anna go with him to the bank and sign the card. Can't find out what's inside until we do."

Ryan nodded agreement and turned to Del. "She ready to go back in the lion's den?"

"She's a trooper, Kevin, accompanied by a woman's curiosity."

"Depending on eventual legal decisions, she might also be the rightful heir to a million bucks," Dutton pointed out.

"Never thought of that," Del said with surprise. "Maybe she's become the lucky one."

"Seems to run in your family," Dutton said. "We also need to explore possible violations regarding smuggling of the ivory tusks. I believe there was an international treaty signed some twenty or thirty years ago to crack down on the trade. I remember reading an article in *National Geographic* that described the slaughter of over 30,000 African elephants each year. Poachers kill the elephants for their tusks, and most of the ivory goes to China. Would you believe that a pair of ivory chop sticks can bring $1,000? Check it out, Kevin."

"Yes, sir. We've got a lot of things cooking."

"And," Dutton interjected, "not enough manpower, right? So, what's new? It's been that way as long as I've been in the Bureau."

"I'm not complaining, boss. Just observing."

"I know, Kevin. You've been in the same boat in the SEALS."

"Amen. We'll carry out the mission, whatever."

"I'll see if I can borrow a couple of agents from the White Collar Squad," Dutton said. "After all, the health care matter is in their playpen." He looked at Del, who was scribbling industriously on a legal pad. "What are you doing?"

Del looked up and displayed a hand written list. "Just tabulating the jurisdictional areas we're in: Espionage, Extortion, Bribery, Fraud, Obstruction of Justice, and Smuggling."

Dutton smiled. "Good start, Del. In your spare time, check the manual and you'll probably find a dozen more possible violations festering around. We all know we've got a load and a half, so dig in and just do it. What's the next step, Kevin?"

"Nadia and the Russian operative meet at *Morton's* tonight."

"No bug on her, right?"

"Didn't think we could chance it, boss. So we went to plan B."

Dutton waited for Ryan's reply.

"We found two volunteers to do a close FISUR."

"Good. Physical surveillance will document the meet for future action. Who did you recruit?"

Ryan displayed a slight grin. "Cynthia appeared to need a good steak dinner."

"Well deserved, and...?"

"It only seemed logical that her immediate supervisor monitored her performance."

Dutton's smile was broad. "Seems logical to me. Enjoy."

* * *

WASHINGTON, D.C.

The plush eatery was buzzing with scintillating conversation between suited lobbyists and legislators, well-coiffed female aides and casually dressed tourists seeking a memorable meal in a prestige landmark. "I sat right next to the head of the EPA," a burbling matron would later gush to her Nebraska neighbor.

"Mr. Winter" was seated in a thickly padded booth when his guest was escorted to his table. "Nadia," he exclaimed, bouncing to his feet. "You dazzle the room!"

"Thank you. Your old-world charm is refreshing. And how should I address you, Mr. Winter?"

The man leaned close as they took their seats. "Serge or Colonel," he said quietly. "As you wish. We don't need secrets between us."

"No," Nadia was saying as the waiter arrived and inquired if they wished a beverage before announcing the dinner specialties. Nadia ordered a Tom Collins, Volkov a Stoly on the rocks.

"You're not having our native drink?" he queried.

"I want my faculties completely clear for our business discussion, Colonel."

We'll see about that, was his thought. "That's commendable, Nadia," he said. "Makes me even more convinced of your complete loyalty."

If you only knew, comrade.

After serving their drinks, the polished waiter described an array of tempting steaks, a petit filet mignon selected by Nadia, a larger choice for him. Salads and sides were also ordered and, at the waiter's recommendation, they ordered a Gran Marnier soufflé that had to be started to be ready at dessert time. Volkov then returned to business.

* * *

A casually dressed couple across the room seemed engrossed in their meal while subtly monitoring the meeting between Nadia and Mr. Winter.

* * *

"We need that missing link," Volkov told Nadia between bites of salad and gulps of Stoly. "It is vitally important to our cause."

"I'm doing my best, Colonel. I keep telling that to Alexei."

"Maybe he's not as determined as I am for results."

"He's been very persistent."

"Has he made clear what it means to you, and your family?"

"Clearly. Their welfare depends on my performance."

"Exactly. I'm glad you understand. I demand results. Enjoy your meal."

* * *

"She doesn't look very happy," Cynthia Chalmers murmured as she glanced over her wine glass. "Wonder how things look outside?"

* * *

Viktor Markov sat in his Virginia cab outside the Georgetown restaurant with his out-of-service sign illuminated. Other local cabs waited patiently for potentially lucrative well-lubricated patrons.

Across the busy street, Special Agents Moretti and Swanson maintained close observation of Viktor's cab. "Wonder how the steaks taste," Moretti said, biting into a *Subway* sandwich.

"Has to be better," Swanson chuckled, "but we don't have to tip."

* * *

In her apartment, Nadia crawled beneath her sheets and sobbed. When will it end was her final prayer before she fell into a troubled sleep.

* * *

Ryan directed Cynthia Chalmers to debrief Nadia at the earliest opportunity and she responded accordingly, quietly slipping into Nadia's apartment building at eight a.m. the following morning. Nadia was sitting at her small kitchen table, sipping coffee and periodically applying an ice bag against a puffy left eye. Her normally light complexion was splotched with red marks. Her dark brown eyes lacked their usual sparkle.

"What the hell happened?" Cynthia exclaimed. "Did he do this to you?"

Nadia nodded, rotating her head in obvious pain.

"The bastard!" Cynthia said. "I'd like to use a nut cracker on his balls."

"Would you like to hear the noble Colonel in action? I have him on tape," Nadia said, picking up a mini tape.

Cynthia nodded assent, and they listened. The voices were distinct, with a range of grunts, groans, and yells emanating from Volkov. Nadia could be heard pleading, "don't, please, ouch, that hurts." The sounds of slaps were frequent.

"Sick," Cynthia said with disgust as Nadia turned off the tape player. "The sonofabitch will pay for this," she vowed, caressing Nadia's heaving shoulders.

Chapter Twenty-five

WASHINGTON, D.C.

Congressman Walters was awakened by his musical alarm at 6:45 a.m. He loved the words of the tune, *This Land is Your Land, This Land is My Land.* *Let's see if my Asian flower is friendlier after she sees what's in the box* was his earliest thought.

FALLS CHURCH, VA

Anna became alert at 7 a.m. when she heard Del's shower water running. She proceeded to join him in what had become an eye-opening ritual. "Wash your back?" she whispered in his ear.

"At least," he gasped. "Good morning, angel."

"How much time do we have before I meet the creep?"

"Enough," he sighed, guiding her hands.

ROCKVILLE, MD

Anna was seated in the foyer of a Bank of America branch in the Washington suburb when the Congressman walked in at 10:15 a.m., wearing casual slacks and jacket and carrying a large briefcase. "Waiting long?" he asked.

"Not too long. I arrived at ten, like you said. Taxis are unpredictable, you know."

"Sorry, but I believe you'll find it worth waiting for. I see you came prepared," he said, gazing at her oversize handbag.

"And there's a large tote bag inside. Yes, I believe I'm prepared."

"Good. Let's see the vault teller."

Walters displayed his safe deposit box key and New Jersey driver's license to the bank officer. Anna showed her still valid Washington, D.C. driver's license from the time she lived in Georgetown. The business-like teller produced the sign-in card for their signatures and opened a locked gate into the vault area. She led them to a numbered box on the bottom row, explaining that was where the largest and heaviest were stored—"and yours is one of the largest we have."

Inserting her and Walters' keys, she opened the outer door to reveal their box. "It's heavy," she said, enlisting Walters help in carrying it to a small windowless room containing a table, two chairs, and an overhead light. They placed the box atop the table. "I assume you wish to be alone," she said.

"Yes, we will need a few minutes," Walters replied.

"Take your time. I'll be nearby to let you out of the vault area when you're finished," she said, closing the door.

Walters' eyes beamed as he opened the box. "Manna from Heaven," he exclaimed, an almost maniacal expression on his face.

"It is an awesome sight," Anna stammered, looking at the stacks of U.S. currency.

"And it's all ours, Anna! Let's spread it out on the table and start counting—two portions."

Walters seemed trance-like as he enthusiastically pulled stacks of $100 Federal Reserve Bank Notes out, reaching ever further back into the fire-resistant container and handing the bills to Anna. Then he suddenly stopped, holding a packet of $500 Bank Notes. "What the hell!"

"What's the matter?" Anna asked. "Are they counterfeit or something?"

Walters sat in one of the chairs, puzzlement clouding his face. "No, they're good, but I just remembered what happened. The Chairman and I had so much cash we couldn't get it all into one safe deposit box in $100 bills so he managed to locate a bunch of $500 bills, and we stuffed it all into this one box. He had some great contacts, you know—some in the Treasury Department."

Anna nodded. "I know he had powerful friends everywhere."

"Yeah, they used to print $500, one thousand, five thousand, and ten thousand notes until about 1946, and stopped circulating them about twenty years later. But they're still good."

"That's good news," Anna commented.

Walters grinned. "Even better than good. I have friends who deal with collectors, and they buy them for more than face value—we've got more than two million here! This is our lucky day! And we share, so you can end up with more than a million, isn't that great?"

Anna nodded. "Great if your friends come through. I'll need to depend on you and them to receive my share."

Walters looked disappointed. "You don't trust me?"

Anna smiled. "It's not that, Jason, but a girl has to look out for her interests. The Chairman always told me that, and he often repeated Reagan's 'Trust but Verify' slogan."

"He was a tough guy," Walters conceded.

"So, let's not worry about that now. Jason. Let's agree we trust each other and get on with our counting. Neither of us wants to be, pardon the expression, "screwed.""

"Don't be too sure about that," Walters muttered as they proceeded to lay out the stacks of bills.

Five minutes later they viewed the separate piles. "I've done some figuring," Walters said. "Each of us gets 50 packets of $100 bills, each packet worth $10,000, for a total of a half million dollars. Each of us also gets ten packets of $500 bills, each worth $50,000 for a total of another half million. A total of one million each. Okay?"

Anna did some quick mental calculations. "Sounds okay. Let's start packing."

Walters said, "Our 60 packets weigh about two ounces each, 120 ounces, or seven and a half pounds for each of us. Not very heavy, but kind of bulky. Can you handle it?"

"Watch me," Anna replied, opening her large handbag and extracting a large canvas tote bag. And, if that doesn't hold it you'll see a woman with the biggest bust in Rockville."

"I'd like to see that," Walters admitted as he began loading his briefcase. "And if that's not enough for me, you might see the biggest boner in town."

"I don't think I'd like to see that, Jason. Keep stuffing your briefcase."

Everything packed, they checked the box again, grabbed their bags and opened the door to call for the vault supervisor. "We're through here, and appreciate the good service," Walters said, surrendering his key. " We won't be needing the box any longer. Moving out of town," he added as they strode away.

"I'll be in touch soon," Walters said as they left the bank and he headed for his black Buick parked around the corner. "Best not to be seen together with this much cash."

Watching from across the street to document the event was Del in a nondescript Chevy Malibu.

Another surveillance car, manned by Moretti and Swanson, started up to follow Walters to his next destination, which turned out to be a Wells Fargo bank in the Watergate complex.

Del closely followed the cab Anna hailed outside the Rockville bank, and they were soon in the Tysons Corner FBI office with Kevin Ryan and a clerical supervisor, counting and identifying the evidence for future proceedings.

ASAC Dutton dropped in and studied the array of bills. "Looks like kidnap ransom," he said, recalling previous cases in his long service. "Photograph them all, with serial numbers clearly visible. It'll help track them when Walters moves the money to his cohorts, especially the two unknown congressional colleagues. And, arrange for the Lab experts to apply their invisible dye to the bills, particularly the $500 ones, so we can further trace their routes." He rubbed his hands together and shook his head. "Not nickel and dime stuff! This is going to be fun," he said on the way out of the room.

"You did good, my million-dollar-baby," Del praised Anna.

"Treat me right, Special Agent Dickerson. I may be worth even more than a million."

Ryan chimed in. "She could be right. The courts might decide she's the legal heir to the whole mess—two million or more."

Anna grinned at Del. "Any response?"

"I know what side my bread is buttered on. What would my lovely princess wish me to do?"

"Just love me," she said quietly as the group returned to reality.

Chapter Twenty-six

Alexei Nikolay's call to Nadia came as a surprise after the previous night's ordeal. "What do you want?" she asked.

"For you to go to work and get the necessary information. What are you doing at home?"

Nadia snickered. "Like this?" she asked, studying her reflection in a wall mirror.

"What do you mean? What's wrong with you? You looked fine the last time I saw you."

"That's before I went out to dinner with your respected Colonel."

"<u>Our</u> Colonel," Nikolay clarified. "He's the boss of both of us."

"Whatever, Alexei. He left a lasting impression, you might say. I can't go out in public for a few days."

"What happened?"

Nadia's tone was bitter. "He demonstrated his manhood, Alexei. He beat the shit out of me."

"He what? That's hard to believe. He's usually calm and collected. Did he drink a lot?"

"He sure did. Plenty of vodka. But that's no excuse. He was a beast."

"Sorry to hear that," Nikolay said. "You know his last name means wolf in English."

"It fits," Nadia said. "Animal."

"Well," Nikolay pursued, "he still expects results, and he mentioned something about us being invited back to Moscow for 'commitment upgrading.'"

"Subtle as a sledgehammer, Alexei. Probably with a one-way ticket."

"He's getting a lot of pressure, Nadia. Did you do something to aggravate him?"

"Khui," (Prick) Nadia cursed. "Always the woman's fault."

"You do need to remember your place."

"Mudak," (Asshole) Nadia said, slamming down the phone.

TYSONS CORNER

Cynthia Chalmers was informing Kevin Ryan of Nadia's assault when Curt Oswald walked in. He listened to the details with escalating facial flushing. "That's disgusting," he fumed. "I'd like to meet the bastard in a remote location."

Ryan's look was grim. "Not only do we owe Nadia safety, but you have to wonder how long her cooperation with us will last."

"I don't have any question about that," Oswald stated. "She's a gallant woman, and committed to securing the freedom of her grandparents. But I'm sure she could use some more encouragement and moral support."

"Cynthia and Del are assigned to her protection," Ryan reminded," but Del's pretty much tied up with the money laundering and bribery situation between Anna and the Congressman."

"I have some free time," Oswald said, "and we seem to have a number of common interests. Maybe I should offer a sympathetic shoulder."

Ryan nodded agreement. "Put your seminary skills to work. Sounds like a good game plan. Go for it."

FALLS CHURCH

Nadia had just swallowed two extra-strength Tylenol tablets when Oswald reached her on her secure cell phone. "Nice to hear a friendly male voice," she said.

"I just heard what happened, Nadia, and am so sorry. You were not supposed to experience such treatment."

Nadia managed a slight laugh. "Unintended consequences, Curt. I wasn't, what's the phrase? promised a rose garden."

"I'd like to see you, Nadia. It might be good to discuss things with a friendly ear."

"I would like that. I'm feeling kind of low right now."

"How about us taking a little ride in the country? I'd like to show you something."

"I've heard of being taken for a ride. Am I coming back?" she laughed.

"Guaranteed. Why don't you get dressed casually, wear some walking shoes, and meet me out front in thirty minutes. I'll be in a black Chevy SUV with tinted windows. Virginia plates."

"All right," she said in a happier voice. "I feel better already. See you soon."

* * *

Nadia wore dark glasses and a pale blue hoodie when she slipped into Oswald's vehicle. "I feel like I'm skipping school," she said, attaching her seat belt.

"We'll continue your education outside of class, Nadia. I'm glad to see you, and again apologize for your trauma."

"No pain, no gain?" she said in a light manner.

"The gain will be substantial, I'm certain. What did you tell your employer about your absence?"

"Just that I needed a couple of sick days—no details. They only pay me for time on the job, so they weren't too upset, but hoped for my early return."

Oswald headed the SUV southbound onto the Washington Beltway and chuckled. "A bit ironic, isn't it, that the guy who is so frantic to secure the missile intelligence is the reason you can't go to the Embassy to get the info because of what he did to you?"

Nadia shared his laugh. "Guess there is some poetic justice. Let the bastard stew in his vodka for a while. By the way, where are we going?"

"Relax, young lady. You'll soon find out. And, for the record, you still look devastating behind your disguise."

"Devastating might be the wrong word," Nadia said, removing her glasses, and turning full–faced toward him, revealing swollen lips, a puffy right eye, and numerous reddish welts.

Oswald took a quick glance. "Still devastating," he asserted, patting Nadia's knee.

Thirty minutes later, Oswald pulled into the parking area of the National Museum of the Marine Corps, just off I-95 in Triangle, Virginia, near the entrance gates of Quantico. "We're here," he proudly announced, pointing at the soaring structure incorporating the image of the famed flag-raisers of Iwo Jima.

"Oh my!" Nadia exclaimed. "It's gorgeous! I've read about it, and always wanted to see it. What a treat."

* * *

After two hours' viewing of the dynamic interactive exhibits depicting Marine Corps history, Nadia and Oswald emerged with glowing tributes to the exceptional museum. "What a source of pride," Nadia enthused. "Makes me additionally determined to become a citizen of your great country."

"You're a natural," Oswald affirmed. "Now, I have another memorable location to show you."

"What a delightful sick day," Nadia said, grasping his arm as they walked to his car.

Several minutes later Oswald was parking in front of the *Globe and Laurel* restaurant on Route 1 in nearby Stafford, Virginia, two miles south of the main gate of Marine Corps Base Quantico. "Another historic gem," Oswald said. "Wait till you see the interior."

"You're overwhelming me," Nadia confessed, looking at the clubby interior jammed with Marine Corps photographs, flags, and other artifacts. "Wow!"

"It's a favorite of current and former Marines, as well as FBI personnel. They have a strong bond, you know. The FBI Academy is on the Quantico base. Students and staff spend considerable off time here."

"I can see why," Nadia said as a hostess welcomed them and led them to a table. They ordered one of the daily lunch specials and proceeded to devour the meal with zest. "Wonderful," Nadia complimented.

"One more thing to show you," Oswald said, rising to guide Nadia to an adjoining private dining room. "Behold the J. Edgar Hoover Room," Oswald announced, leading Nadia into the banquet room packed with FBI memorabilia, including numerous photographs and sketches of the legendary FBI Director. "The Quantico Chapter of the Former FBI Agents Society meet here regularly, and many new agents graduating from the Academy celebrate here with their families. It's like a home away from home."

"You have outdone yourself, Curt. What a morale booster this day has been."

"These are things that give me inspiration," Oswald commented softly.

"Well, you've inspired me, Curt. Thanks. I was thinking of going to a service at my new church tonight for spiritual support."

"That sounds healthy," the former seminarian said, looking at his watch. "It's fairly early, if you still want to attend. We're only about an hour away."

"That would make it a perfect day," Nadia pondered, "but I feel a bit apprehensive driving in heavy traffic with restricted vision in one eye."

"I'd be happy to take you there," Oswald said after a short pause.

Nadia's eyes flashed. "You would?" She reached out and squeezed Oswald's hand. "You're a good man."

Chapter Twenty-seven

FAIRFAX, VA

Approximately seventy worshipers gathered in the sanctuary of the new and growing Russian congregation. Religious icons adorned the walls, and the energetic pastor led congregants in prayer. Oswald sat quietly beside Nadia who appeared absorbed in the spiritual essence. The encouraging words of the articulate clergyman in a homily loaded with hope and potential seemed to further elevate her spirits.

During a brief social session after the service, Nadia discreetly pointed to a middle-aged woman engaged in discussion with two other women. "She works in the Russian Embassy Annex. Let's ease our way out."

* * *

FALLS CHURCH

"What a memorable day," Nadia said as they pulled up at her apartment building at nine thirty p.m. "You've restored me, Curt."

"It's rewarding to see you revived, Nadia, and you can feel confident that there are better days ahead. I'm sure you're exhausted from our outing, so I'll say goodnight here and wish you a sound sleep."

Nadia smiled and moved closer to kiss his cheek. "You <u>are</u> a good man, Curt."

"I try, but I'm only human, you should be aware."

"Thanks for the warning. I'm trained in Tae Kwon Do, you know."

"In what? Oh, the martial arts you've been sharing with Del. I heard about what happened to him. Why didn't you use it on the Colonel?"

"In time," Nadia said. "It could have disrupted the whole operation, but you can bet your Yankee dollar that Nadia doesn't forget."

* * *

Her home phone was ringing when Nadia entered her apartment. "Where have you been?" the angry voice of Alexei Nikolay demanded. "I've been trying to reach you all afternoon."

"Out, trying to forget what happened last night."

"Well, you should have told me where you were."

"Why? So you could beat me up, too?"

"I wouldn't do that, Nadia."

"You can bet on that, Alexei. I'd crunch your nuts."

"You can be very descriptive."

"Just pray you don't find out. So, what do you want?"

"The date you can get back to work. The Colonel keeps bugging me."

"Hah, doesn't the pig understand he's the reason I'm not at work?"

"I believe he does. He's getting a lot of heat from his superiors."

"Poor bastard. I really feel sorry for him. Wait while I pull out another Kleenex."

"We have to think of the welfare of our country, Nadia, and, I might remind you, the wellbeing of family members."

"I never forget that, Alexei. Tell your friend I'll see how I look in the morning. I'll let you know."

"Oh," Nikolay said with unconvincing casualness, "I received a call from a patriot. She thought she saw you tonight."

"Well, isn't that lovely. Spying on me again."

"It wasn't spying, just some interesting information about your activities."

"I was in church, for Christ's sake! You ought to try it."

"Listening to a man who left his country. He could be dangerous."

"Everyone knows I'm a Christian. Our leaders have been happy to employ my talents regardless."

"Yes, it's been an unusual arrangement."

"So, do you want to dispense with my services?"

"No, no. I'm not suggesting that, just reminding you where you welfare rests."

"Thanks for your understanding, Alexei. I'm overwhelmed by your concern."

"Let's not be sarcastic, Nadia. And, I don't want to pry, but who was the guy you were with?"

"Just a friendly man I met at church," she said after a skipped heartbeat.

TYSONS CORNER

Oswald was in Kevin Ryan's FBI office early the following morning when he received a call from Nadia. "Someone working at the Russian Embassy Annex saw us at church last night. She reported it to Alexei, and he called me. Wants to know who you are."

"I'm with Kevin," Oswald interjected. "Let me put you on his speaker. Okay, what did you tell him?"

"That you were just a friendly man I met at church."

"Sounds right, but I see the concern. We need to be doubly careful in our contacts."

"He wants to know when I'm going back to work."

"And, you said?"

"That I'd check my appearance. I could use a lot of makeup, and tell my employer that I tripped over something and fell on my face. I believe there's a meeting scheduled with the important high-tech missile experts that will need translating. It might be the opportunity to identify their connections."

Ryan entered the conversation. "We're relying on your judgement, Nadia. Curt told me about your outing yesterday, and we're most grateful for your sacrifices. Your wellbeing is a prime concern, as are the risks to you. So, we will leave it up to you when you return to the firing line."

"I like that firing line phrase, Kevin, and since I'm in the mood to shoot someone, I'll call the embassy and tell them I'll be in tomorrow. That okay?"

"Sounds like a winner. And Curt is saying something in a foreign language that I don't understand."

"Spaseeba," (Thank you) Oswald said.

"Pazhalooysta," (You're welcome) Nadia replied.

Chapter Twenty-eight

<u>WASHINGTON, D.C.</u>

The voice of Congressman Jason Walters was velvety. "I hope you are well this lovely morning, Anna."

"I'm feeling great, Jason, and hope that you are too."

"Couldn't be better, and ready to learn the value of those surprise items we discovered."

"Yes, I too am curious."

"I'm assuming you have your segment safely secured."

"I believe so."

"How about that insurance salesman? Does he know about your good fortune?"

"I believe that some things should remain secret."

"Good. Prosperity can sometimes instigate base instincts. I've scheduled a meeting with one of my valued contacts to explore the market for the special items, and thought it only fair to include some from your collection—say ten or so to start. What do you think?"

"You are more familiar with such things, so I will defer to your judgement. Will you be using some of yours too?"

"Yes, an equal number. I want us to be partners in this endeavor, Anna. And, not to pry, but I trust you have not placed your collection under your mattress."

"You can be sure of that. I believe it is in a safe place. And, not to pry in return, how about you?"

"I like your frankness, Anna. Let me just say I believe in strong facilities."

"Fair enough, Jason. How do I deliver my items to you?"

"After a stressful day dealing with the Nation's problems, it is good to relax. How about dinner at my place? Our building restaurant caters excellent meals. We can discuss business and satisfy our hungers at the same time."

I'm sure I know what you're thinking of, Anna thought. "I can arrange that," she said. "What day and time?"

"The sooner the better, Anna. It will be exciting to explore how fortunate we are. Tomorrow evening at seven?"

"I'll be there, Jason."

And I'll be ready to explore you, Walters mused as he cradled his phone.

TYSONS CORNER

Anna and Del were in Kevin Ryan's office debating the next steps. "Here are the treated $500 bills," Ryan said, handing the small packet to Anna. "We're depending on these little rascals to lead us to the money launderers and corrupt legislators. They've been checked out of the evidence vault, even though they might be eventually determined to be legally yours."

"I don't plan on spending any of it," Anna said.

"Not even on the pitiful insurance salesman?" Del joked.

"Poor boy, he gets no respect," Anna laughed in return.

"You'll need to be prepared for his, what's the term, amorous advances?" Ryan cautioned.

"Damn, I hate to put you in the clutches of that snake," Del muttered.

"Don't worry," Anna consoled. "I've dealt with reptiles before. I have a plan."

* * *

Anna and Del were seated in the fashionable *Clyde's* restaurant in McLean, enjoying one of its signature prime rib dinners. Anna sighed contentedly as she placed her fork on her empty plate. "If you don't stop treating me to this fancy life, I'll need to get a larger-size wardrobe."

Del nodded. "I know what you mean. I'll need to move faster at tomorrow's Tae Kwon Do session to work off all these calories."

"You and Nadia," Anna said. "She seems to be able to maintain her figure."

"Yeah, she's very energetic."

"Do you enjoy exercising with her?"

"She's a pleasant opponent," Del said, sensing the direction of the conversation.

"And beautiful."

"Not as beautiful as you, Anna. I thought we already agreed on that."

Anna paused. "I'm sorry, honey, I know I shouldn't be bugging you about that, but you know how women are."

"Wonderful creatures," Del said, picking up his wine glass and clinking it against hers.

Anna drained her glass. "Just don't forget where to burn your calories," she said with a demure smile.

***

Three miles away, Nadia was ending a terse phone conversation with Alexei. "I'm going to work tomorrow, you can inform your favorite Colonel. And no, I don't think Dickerson is on to me. He's too dumb. I expect to see him at the Tae Kwon Do studio tomorrow evening. Don't worry about him. I think you and the Colonel are overreacting."

A frown creased her face when she put her phone down. *They're getting too close to learning the truth about Del. I need to warn him.*

Chapter Twenty-nine

Nadia's day was productive. Her translating skills were required concerning some engineering drawings provided by the missile scientists to her employer the previous day. She was certain her Russian handlers would be elated, no less so than her American overseers who had supplied the critical misinformation that would eventually result in disastrous failure of a monstrous weapon of destruction. Pondering the significance of her double identity roles, Nadia couldn't suppress a small smile. Rather exciting. Can't wait to tell Del tonight.

* * *

Del drove Anna to Rosslyn on the Virginia side of the Key Bridge where she would catch a cab to Walters' Watergate apartment building. "I still have negative feelings about subjecting you to this, Anna. I should be doing the dirty work."

"You'll get your turn," she consoled. "Let me have a little excitement."

"You sure you can handle the jerk? You know what he wants."

"I'm sure," Anna said, kissing his cheek before exiting his car. "You can hear his line on the little bug Cynthia just helped me install."

"Well, I'm still worrying. Be careful."

"Always, dear. See you after."

* * *

Walters greeted Anna with an exuberant hug at the door of his luxurious apartment. "You look ravishing," he declared as his eyes traveled over her snug beige two-piece suit. His look lingered on the appealing décolletage of her ruffled pink silk blouse. "I took the liberty of dressing casually, Anna, sort of the homey effect."

"You look at home," she said, gazing at his embroidered silk smoking jacket. Shades of Hugh Hefner, she thought. Where's the pipe?

"I was enjoying a Manhattan. May I offer you the same, or something else?"

"A glass of white wine would be perfect, Jason. I'm not much of a drinker."

"You need to explore new delights, Anna, with the benefits you have recently come into."

"I'll think about it," she said, watching him fill an oversize goblet with chardonnay.

"Before we get down to business, let me show you the view," he said, leading her into a large bedroom with a wide sliding door. Looking out, she viewed the flowing Potomac River several floors below.

"Very impressive," she said with enthusiasm.

"I love to wake up to the sound of the river," he said, glancing at the King-sized bed that Anna noted had the cover turned down.

"You live well, Jason."

"As you will too, Anna, especially with the bonus we discovered. Did you bring the bills?"

"Definitely. They're in my purse. I left it in the living room. Let me get it."

"Yes," Walters said. We'll get to this later, was his thought.

Anna offered a silent prayer as they moved back to the living room. I hope this is all being recorded.

"Here they are," she said, "and tell me again how you will cash them in."

"My contacts, Anna. They can't wait to get their hands on them."

"Do they have names?"

Walters laughed. "Of course, but you don't have to worry about such details. Trust me."

"Certainly, Jason. You know how curious women can be. It's our nature."

"And nature has been good to you, Anna. You are a very desirable woman, you know. Wouldn't you be more comfortable with your jacket off?"

"Well, I am a little warm," she said, standing to remove the garment.

"Pretty blouse," Walters said. "It flatters your lovely figure."

"Thanks, but I feel obligated to remind you that I'm engaged."

"To that insurance salesman."

"Yes."

"Do you think he really appreciates you? You could be traveling again in powerful circles."

"He's a nice guy."

"There are lots of nice guys out there—some of them better able to give you excitement and exposure to the elite life."

"That's food for thought, Jason."

"Speaking of food, I ordered chicken cordon bleu from the *Kingbird* restaurant in the building. It's one of their specialties. Okay?"

"Whatever you say. I'm easy to please."

"Meanwhile, how about another drink?" Walters said, mixing another oversize Manhattan.

"Just a little. You poured me a large glass to start."

"It helps us relax," he said, sitting next to her on a white leather couch and draping an arm over her shoulder.

Anna searched for a diversion. "Tell me about your other businesses."

"Well, I rather wound down after the Chairman died, except for the one we're engaged in, but I have heavy congressional duties that keep me very busy."

"I don't know how you do it all, Jason. You have to be very smart."

"And have cooperative friends," he followed with a self-satisfied smile.

"That takes a lot of skill. You must be a great negotiator in your state."

Walters took a large sip of his drink. "Not just in my state. I've got good friends all over."

"I can see that with your personality you'd get along well with men."

"Not only men, my dear," he said after another sip.

"No, of course not. You can charm both sexes."

"I hope so," he was saying when the room service waiter arrived with their meal.

Anna pondered how far she should press on identifying his potential bribe-prone colleagues, electing to limit her questions as she watched him wash down his meal with generous gulps of dinner wine. She also noticed his eyes becoming increasingly blurry.

"I can see a glorious future for us," he said, staggering to his feet. "I've got to go to the little boy's room," he giggled. "Meanwhile, we need an after-dinner drink," he said, pointing to his well-stocked bar. "Grand Marnier for me. You fix. Bring it into the bedroom. It's celebration time!"

As Walters lurched on unsteady feet from the room, Anna approached the bar and filled a snifter with the amber-colored cordial. She then extracted a small paper packet from her purse, tore it open, and dropped its contents into the glass, pleased to see how swiftly it dissolved. She carried the goblet into the bedroom, along with her wine glass.

Walters emerged from the bathroom, sans smoking jacket, and grabbed the proffered glass. "Time for action," he declared, gulping down the contents. "Get undressed!"

Anna looked into his blazing eyes and slowly placed her glass on a bedside table. With a subtle smile she began to unbutton her blouse.

Walters' heavy breathing was audible as he watched the fabric parting to reveal Anna's lace-trimmed red bra, struggling to constrain her rounded breasts.

Walters' eyes bulged. "At last!" he exclaimed, seconds before he clutched his stomach and fell to the floor.

Anna studied her host writhing on the plush white carpet before he suddenly emptied the contents of his stomach and passed out. "Poor boy," Anna murmured, re-buttoning her blouse. "It really is good to have friends. Thanks, Nadia."

* * *

Fifteen minutes later Anna stood troubled at the curbside entrance of the Watergate, wondering where Del was, and why he hadn't answered her repeated cell phone calls as she left Walters' apartment. An emergency must have occurred, she concluded before hailing a cab to return her to the Westin. I'm sure there's an explanation, was her concerned thought.

* * *

Nadia left the Tae Kwon Do studio after the evening session, puzzled why Del had failed to show up as scheduled. Something unexpected happened, she reasoned. But he usually calls, was her disquieting feeling as she headed home.

* * *

Where am I? Special Agent Del Dickerson wondered as he regained consciousness on the dirt floor of a dank room. And where are my clothes? The evaporating scent of chloroform wafted through the silent darkness.

Chapter Thirty

TYSONS CORNER

Anna's call to Kevin Ryan sounded frantic. "He's not at the Westin. No message. I tried to call his cell number—no answer. I'm worried sick!"

"Keep calm, Anna," Ryan comforted. "We all know he is occasionally unpredictable, but he's a survivor. I'm sure he's okay. Cynthia's on her way to be with you. By the way, how did it go with the Congressman? Hate to ask at this time, but Dutton will want to know."

"Very well, I believe. Cynthia will be able to hear what the bug picked up. But I'm so worried, Kevin."

"Stay strong, and think positive, Anna."

* * *

Ryan's next call had him thinking less positive when Nadia asked if Del had been sent somewhere else since he hadn't been at the Tae Kwon Do session.

"Not to my knowledge, Nadia, but don't worry, I'm sure there's a good explanation. I'll get back to you," he said with growing apprehension.

* * *

"So where the hell is he?" ASAC Andy Dutton questioned, listening to Ryan and glancing at his den clock. "It's almost midnight. Even he can't just disappear. Did you try his cell?"

"First thing, boss. No answer. So did Anna and Nadia try with no luck."

"What about his car? Any sighting?"

"My next check, Andy."

"You still at the office, Kevin?"

"No, got home about an hour ago."

"You enjoying your nine to five job?"

"Yeah, like we had in the SEALS."

"What did you tell me was one of your mottos, *'The Only Easy Day Was Yesterday'*?"

"You got it, boss. I'll let you know what I find out."

* * *

Ryan's call to the car rental agency offered a ray of hope. "It has a GPS unit," the rental clerk informed. "Let me check." Following Ryan's two minutes of finger-tapping phone holding, the clerk returned. "It's currently on Columbia Pike in Annandale," he said, providing the street address.

Ryan immediately ordered a roving FBI surveillance unit in the area to check it out and called Dutton. "Maybe he's taking a nap," Dutton joked weakly.

Ten minutes later, an agent from the surveillance unit reported back to Ryan. "The car is in the parking lot of the Tae Kwon Do martial arts studio which is closed. Driver's door unlocked. Keys in ignition. Nothing inside the vehicle except a strong chemical odor—smells like chloroform according to my partner who was an EMT. No one in the area."

"Thanks for the quick response," Ryan said. "Lock the car and get the keys to the Evidence Response team I'm sending that way to process it for prints and such."

Ryan relayed the finding to Dutton who told him to gather the "Trappers" at the office the following morning.

"How about Nadia?" Ryan questioned. "She is possibly being watched, so slipping her into the building can be done, but could be risky. Also, if she doesn't appear at work that could raise more suspicions. She already voiced concern about Del's true identity being known to her Russian handlers, putting both of them into possible jeopardy."

"Good thinking," Dutton replied. "Let's keep her in the loop via secure cell line for now, but find out if she recalls seeing Del's car at the studio."

"Will do. What time in the morning?"

Dutton glanced at his clock which read thirty minutes past midnight. "Let's sleep in, Kevin. Make it seven a.m."

* * *

Del's clouded mind slowly cleared as his body shifted on the cold ground. Near total darkness engulfed him. Handcuffs on his wrists limited efforts to sit up. Struggling to upright himself, he discovered he was naked except for his Jockey shorts and socks.

Recollections filtered back, and he slowly reviewed his last conscious actions. While parking at the Annandale Tae Kwon Do studio, he observed that Nadia's car was already there. Then a white van pulled alongside him and a man jumped out and rushed to open his hood. "Help!" he called out. "It's on fire!"

Del recalled leaping out to peer into the engine compartment, turning back in puzzlement when he saw no flames, only to feel a damp cloth forced over his face. There was a vague recollection of struggling against strong arms, then oblivion until his recent awakening.

Now, as he sat in the darkness, he saw a sliver of dim light on a wall opposite him. Straining to focus, he thought he detected the outline of a door, the line of light apparently on its jamb. Struggling to his feet, he moved to the light source and ran his handcuffed hands over the edges of a wooden door which felt solid and unmoving. He discovered a metal handle, likewise sturdy and unmovable.

Where the hell am I, Del wondered.

"Hello!" he called out.

Silence followed.

"Help!" he called out again. The lack of response was dispiriting as silence prevailed.

With his eyes adjusting to a limited degree from the doorway's strip of light, Del examined his surroundings. Moving cautiously, he discovered a room he estimated to be approximately twelve by twenty feet. Empty wooden shelves lined two walls. Against a third wall he stumbled over a narrow cot. Exploring fingers indicated it was a folding military-style cot, equipped with a coarse blanket. No pillow.

Completing his perimeter search, he moved slowly toward the center of the room where he found in the dimness a wooden table with a roughly three by three foot top. A straight wooden chair stood nearby. All the comforts of home, Del snickered. Wonder what time it is? Striving to see his wrists in the dimness proved futile. His watch was gone.

Well, not much else to do, he concluded, carefully moving to the cot and curling up under the rough blanket that smelled of mothballs.

TYSONS CORNER

"Nadia told me his car was not there when she arrived, and she didn't see it when she left," Ryan reported to the bleary-eyed group assembled in Dutton's conference room. "That sounded strange, so I quizzed her further. She said there are two sections of parking at the studio, one out of sight of the other. I checked with the surveillance unit that found the car. It was parked in the other section that she couldn't see."

"Which means it was moved," Oswald said.

"Right," Ryan replied, "which encouraged the Evidence Response team to find Del's prints on the steering wheel of his car, along with some additional latent prints that Ident is trying to identify. That may tell us who moved the car."

"And who may be responsible for his disappearance," Dutton noted.

Anna sat quietly in a state of near shock. "I'm so worried," she said somberly.

"We all are," Dutton consoled, "but rest assured we're proceeding all out on getting him back safe and sound. I talked with Assistant Director Wayne Jackson a few minutes ago. He said the Director has Del's recovery a top Bureau priority. We won't let a stone be uncovered. And," he added with a gentle smile, "we are all aware of his legendary luck."

Anna managed a weak smile.

Dutton continued. "Kevin filled me in on your outstanding work in handling Walters and eliciting valuable leads in identifying his congressional colleagues who are possibly receptive to bribes—a close friend in another state and a woman. Two fitting those rough limitations have been on our radar for some time. I believe we're getting close to pinpointing who they are, along with learning who his money-laundering contacts are. You performed admirably."

After a brief pause, Dutton went on. "I know it's asking a lot, but do you feel up to maintaining the effort with Walters? I know your latest encounter was, ah, unpleasant."

Anna nodded, then raised her chin and spoke with determination. "Of course. It's what Del would do for me. He's my life."

"I salute you," Dutton said. "He'll be back, and I'm sure he'll have a tale to tell."

"Speaking of tales to tell," Anna said in a more upbeat tone, "I need to call Jason and inquire about his health."

Light laughter rumbled among the group.

WASHINGTON, D.C.

Anna's call to the congressional office of the Honorable Jason Walters was put directly through on his personal line.

"What the hell happened?" he asked. "I woke up on the floor and you were gone."

"It was such a shock, Jason. You just suddenly got sick and collapsed. I didn't know what to do. I considered calling 911."

"Good thing you didn't," Walters hurried to say. "Damned reporters go wild over such things."

"When I couldn't wake you up, I placed your head on a pillow and covered you with a blanket."

"Thanks for that. It must have been that damned chicken. I'll have some strong words with the chef. It ruined our evening."

"Yes, I was so disappointed."

"Well, we'll make up for it. I've sent the items we discussed by courier to one of my contacts, and I'll let you know what he says."

"I'm anxious to know, Jason, and to see you again."

"Likewise, Anna. We have a lot of unfinished business."

Chapter Thirty-one

Del's eyes slowly opened when he heard sounds of movement above. Faint light from a small window high on one wall partially illuminated the room. The window that he guessed was about twelve by eighteen inches was thickly covered with dusty grime and cobwebs. Looking up, he saw a small lightbulb centered in the ceiling. No light switch was visible on a wall. The walls appeared to be of field stones cemented together. Resembles a root or wine cellar, he thought, momentarily recalling the wine cellar he was trapped in in the Sierra Nevada Mountains a few years before. Got out of that alive, he remembered with elevated spirits.

The sound of shuffling feet redirected his attention upward to the thick wooden beams supporting the ceiling. Old, he judged. Two metal supporting poles were spaced equidistant apart in the room. What appeared to be a porta-potty sat in a distant corner.

Concluding that action was needed, Del yelled "HELLO! IS ANYONE THERE?"

No verbal response resulted, but more foot shuffling was heard. A faint aroma of frying food reminded Del he had not eaten lately.

"HELLO!" he tried again, louder. No reply.

Save your breath, Del concluded. Figure how to get out of this place. Closely eyeing the Peerless handcuffs encasing his wrists, he chuckled. They look like mine. Wish I had my key.

After using the porta-potty that appeared to be new, he utilized the increasing light to examine the walls, determining that the sturdy wood door was the only opening other than the small out-of-reach window. Boy Scout and FBI training lessons flowed through his mind in search of escape possibilities.

Several minutes passed before he was startled to see the overhead lightbulb illuminate. Low power, Del noted—probably 40-watts he guessed. The relative brightness was followed by an accented voice from a speaker concealed behind a floor joist. "Stand away from the door if you want something to eat—at least two meters."

Foreign measure, Del noted as he calculated the distance in feet and stepped back about seven feet. "I'm doing it," he quickly answered.

A minute later the door opened and two burly men entered, one carrying an automatic pistol, the other a tray that he placed on the table. Both men wore black cloth hoods, with eye, ear, and lip openings. The hoods reached to blue jean shirts.

"What am I doing here?" Del asked. "And who are you?"

"You're a guest," the gunman replied in an accented voice. "It's no business of yours who we are. Just call us your friends."

Del laughed. "Friends do this?" he asked.

"Don't be smart. Be happy that you are still alive."

"Do you have names?" Del asked.

"Not necessary. Eat your food."

"I need to tell my family I'm okay."

"They'll find out."

"Do you know who I am?"

The man who brought the food tray snorted. "We know all about you."

"Then you know you've kidnaped a Federal officer and face life imprisonment, possibly execution."

"Execution?" he asked his partner.

"Don't listen to him," the man with the gun said. "We need to go."

"What do you want from me?" Del implored.

"You'll find out," he said, directing his accomplice toward the door.

"Can't you take these handcuffs off? It's very awkward doing anything. I'm not going anywhere."

"That's for sure. I'll ask the boss."

"Who's the boss?"

"You'll find that out soon. Now, no more questions if you want to keep being fed."

As the men passed through the door, Del noticed the rolled up sleeves of the gunman, and particularly the small tattoo of a flower peering through black hair covering his upper left arm.

A rose? Del speculated.

A second after the thick door closed, there was the sound of a bolt sliding home, and the overhead light was extinguished. Light switch has to be on the outside, Del deduced, moving to the table. Dinner time.

A paper napkin covered the contents of a paper plate that displayed a thick slice of brown bread, a semi-warm sausage, and a banana. A half-pint of milk in a paper carton completed the array. Blue Moon Dairy was imprinted on the container, with no address listed. Also, no utensils. Bon appetit, Del said to himself, settling on the solitary chair and maneuvering his cuffed hands to attack the food.

Chapter Thirty-two

TYSONS CORNER

Andy Dutton and Kevin Ryan were in deep discussion in Dutton's office. "What's your take?" Dutton asked.

"It has to be the Russians. They know who Del is, and they may have concluded he was a threat to their highly valuable spy."

"No chance it could be Walters trying to rid himself of an annoying complication in his plans to win Anna's favors?"

"I considered that, boss, but doubt he would go that far, even if we know what a weasel he is, and that he has unsavory associates capable of doing anything for money."

Dutton nodded. "Yeah, that's pretty much my assessment. Let's concentrate on the Russkie probability. Where do we stand?"

Ryan glanced at the stack of papers he had spread out on his side of Dutton's desk. "Well, Del's last known contact with anyone was a cell phone conversation with Anna about five-thirty p.m. when he said he would pick her up at the Watergate. She was supposed to call him when she left Walters' apartment. Del was heading for his Tae Kwon Do session."

"Where Nadia said she didn't see his car when she arrived, was surprised when he didn't show up, and didn't see his car when she left," Dutton said.

"Right, but we learned from the car rental company that his car was parked in a lot that Nadia couldn't see, and that it had been moved."

"Leaving lots of prints, Kevin, mainly Del's, but some additional latents that Ident is examining."

"It's really a long shot, boss. It's a rental."

"I agree, but we need to pursue it. Do we need to pull Nadia out now, since we've planted the missile bug, and have identified most of the conspirators in the Russian Embassy?"

"Guess those are the decisions ASAC's make," Ryan said with a smile. "But, I do believe we have enough evidence to bounce a lot of their 'diplomats' out of the country, and put a crimp in their network for a while."

"For a while is right, Kevin. The battle goes on. One more ingredient before we pull Nadia out is insuring that our plan to extricate her grandparents is ready. I've been told that our sister Agency has a plan in place, ready to execute when we give the word."

"Lots of food for thought, sir. And from your expression, I suspect that the thought food is not digesting too well."

"You're an astute observer, Kevin. If the Russians have Del, what might they do to discover what we know about Nadia's work for us?"

"I'm reluctant to think about the possibilities—we know their capabilities."

"Yeah, the guy's legendary luck is really needed now. How's Anna doing?"

"Displaying oriental inscrutability, but naturally churning inside. Cynthia is staying with her."

"We also need tight coverage for Nadia, Kevin."

"We have it with Oswald. He seems to have assumed a spiritual-like oversight."

Dutton's expression brightened. "That may be the extra ingredient we have over the Russians—the power of prayer."

"Amen," Ryan concurred.

WASHINGTON, D.C.

"Anna," Jason Walters boomed in a vibrant voice. "I have some great news. My man just called to inform me there's a ten percent premium on the items we discussed."

"That's wonderful, Jason."

"And that's not all, he wants more of the big ones we have."

"You're a terrific businessman."

"There's more. I have to go to a two-day congressional seminar at Williamsburg starting tomorrow. They have a big reception the second night."

"That sounds elegant."

"For damned sure. I want you to go to it with me."

"Ah . . . I'm sort of speechless."

"I understand. It's like the ones you used to go to with the Chairman. You'll meet some of my special colleagues."

"It does sound intriguing."

"You can bring the 'big boys' we talked about. My man lives nearby, and can come to the hotel to pick them up. We're staying at the Williamsburg Inn."

"You are certainly a man of action. How do I get there?"

"Already arranged that. You have a reservation on Amtrak, Business Class, of course. You leave from Union Station at one-thirty and arrive at Williamsburg at five-twenty. Take a cab to the Inn."

"I don't know what to say, Jason."

"Just tell that insurance salesman you have to go visit a sick aunt or something. Can you handle that?"

Anna closed her eyes and offered a silent prayer at the mention of her missing fiancée. "Certainly," she said with conviction, wiping a drop of moisture from an eye.

* * *

Anna's immediate call to Kevin Ryan had everyone energized. "We might be able to identify his money launderer," was Ryan's first reaction.

"And meet some of his special colleagues," Dutton added.

"Ah, always seeing the big picture," Ryan jested. "Guess that's why you're the boss."

"Screw you," Dutton said with a smile, punching Ryan's shoulder. "Call Norfolk. They cover Williamsburg. See if they can lend a couple of agents, and find out what contacts they have in the area. Tell them we need to have Cynthia at the banquet. Things are heating up, my boy."

"Love to be at the scene of action, boss."

"I know what you mean, Kevin. The price we pay for so-called administrative advancement. Wonder how Del is doing?"

SOMEWHERE

Wish I had something to read, Del mused after finishing his meal, random thoughts fleeting through his mind. Sausage was pretty spicy, but the bread was fresh and the banana filling. Visions of his recent prime rib dinner with Anna surfaced. Miss you, honey. Don't worry, we'll get out of this. Have to think positive. Wish I could scratch my back. Damned handcuffs. Sure made it hard to eat. A little music might be elevating, he decided, prompting him to start whistling, a favorite practice since his youth. Patriotic tunes were his favorite, and he smiled inwardly as he recalled how Andy Dutton's dog, Rambo, wagged his imposing tail wildly when he whistled *Yankee Doodle Dandy*. With spirits raised after a half-hour or so of his music repertoire, Del eventually slumped back in the solitary chair. This really sucks, he concluded.

TYSONS CORNER

Ryan was back in Dutton's office following a lengthy conference call with the Norfolk Special Agent in Charge. "Everything looks good," he said. "Two of their top agents are heading that way, along with the Agent from the Newport News Resident Agency who covers the area and reportedly knows everyone in town. He's in the same service club as the Manager of the Williamsburg Inn. Said the Lions Club motto is *We Serve,* and they're more than happy to do just that."

"A good patriotic organization," Dutton replied. "I've spoken at several of their meetings and will probably join when I retire and have more time."

"Charlie Maxwell is the local agent, and will be our main contact there," Ryan advised. "He has liaison with Camp Peary, better known as 'The Farm,' which everyone knows is a major CIA training facility. He's also a Navy vet. Not SEALS, but close enough. EOD. We'll be in good company."

"EOD?"

"Explosive Ordnance Disposal."

Dutton nodded. "That sounds about right. We're sitting on a couple of ticking bombs. We need to defuse them before they explode."

"Isn't that what we're here for?" Ryan remarked, ending their conversation.

FBI Code Name: SPYTRAP

Chapter Thirty-three

<u>SOMEWHERE</u>

Del decided that resting on the cot was more comfortable than the hard wooden chair and was staring at the ceiling when the ceiling light flicked on. He next heard the same accented voice coming from the obscured speaker. "Back from the door," the voice instructed. "You have company."

Seconds later the sound of the dead bolt resounded and the door opened. Both of the same hooded men entered, each carrying pistols, followed by an eye-opening sight. A tall woman, dressed sparsely in black leather strode in. Stiletto heels supporting curvaceous legs raised her height to around six feet. She was masked, but blonde hair curled around its edges. Generous red- glossed lips emerged from the mouth opening. Her eyes appeared to be blue. She carried a black leather whip and a leather bag which she placed on the table. With a gesture to the men, she said, "Around the pole." Del pondered the accent. Slavic?

At the command, one man pulled Del from the cot while the other continued to level his weapon at Del's midsection. One of Del's cuffs was unlocked and he was dragged to one of the metal poles where his hands were cuffed in front of him around the pole. With that, the gunmen stuffed their pistols in their waistbands and looked at the woman.

Del too studied the woman, noting that she was full-figured and wore a minimum of clothing. Indeed, when she moved, cutouts in the leather revealed ample portions of bare flesh, including around her full breasts where rouged nipples prominently protruded. Open slits of leather between her thighs disclosed wisps of curly blonde pubic hair.

Del involuntarily gulped.

The woman strode toward Del and cracked the whip she carried, a resounding sound that caused everyone in the room to jump.

"I am Tanya," she announced in a husky voice. "I am here to gain information. I can give pain or pleasure," she said, cracking the whip again. "Is that clear?"

Del cleared his throat. "Are you the boss?"

"Yes, isn't that obvious?"

"Then you know you are in serious trouble holding a Federal agent captive."

Tanya laughed, and cracked the whip again, its metal-tipped end landing close to Del's feet. "I was told you have a weird sense of humor."

"You're all facing execution, you know."

The woman laughed again, sending another whip tail near his right toe. "You are in no position to threaten me. I'm in charge, and you will do what I ask, or else."

She turned to the men. "Since this pig isn't going anywhere, you may rest outside the door while I interrogate him. My techniques are quite personal, you might say, but to give you an idea let me show you what's in my bag." With another crack of the whip that grazed Del's other foot, Tanya moved to the table and opened the satchel. One by one she extracted a variety of implements—pliers, an ice pick, a file, a small saw, masking tape, razor blades, safety pins, a mallet, a miniature vise, and a small Butane torch.

Good Lord, Del silently prayed. This doesn't look like it will be a good day.

"And," Tanya added, "bring a cushion from that couch in the hallway. Our guest might be doing some reclining. Make that two cushions. We both might be reclining."

With the cushions delivered by the men whose demeanor indicated disappointment, and with the door closing, the woman turned to Del. "Shall we begin?"

* * *

TYSONS CORNER

"Cynthia drove down to Williamsburg and made contact with Maxwell," Ryan informed Dutton. "He has arranged for her to be at the reception, along with the Norfolk agents. They'll be particularly attentive to who Walters huddles with. Anna's aboard the train."

"So we wait," Dutton sighed. "Can't stop wondering where Del is and how he's doing."

"No news, good news, boss?"

"Let's hope and pray so."

SOMEWHERE

"Pain and pleasure are often close to each other," she said loud enough to be heard through the door before again cracking the whip She then astounded Del when she knelt close to him on one of the cushions. "I hope you are a good actor," she whispered. " I am a friend of Nadia's."

Del's emotions soared. "An answer to my prayers. What do you want me to do?"

"Yell, scream, moan and groan every time I pinch you," she said squeezing his thigh.

"OWW!" Del dutifully responded.

The whip cracked again.

Del screamed.

"Louder," she said, pinching his arm.

He tried louder.

"That's better," she said in a low voice. "Nadia said she knew someone who might help get me out of this life. Scream as loud as you can," she added.

Del did his best, adding a loud moan.

"I just came over," she said, "and they are sort of giving me a tryout. They're trying to make me into a monster."

"You certainly look the part," Del said, prompting a loud slap on his cheek, followed by a spontaneous cry from him.

"We need to make you look battered," she said, pinching his chest.

Del howled like a whipped dog.

"They suspect that Nadia might be betraying them. I'm supposed to find out," she said, again cracking the whip.

"Where are we?" Del asked.

"In the basement of a big, old house down a bumpy road."

"But you don't know where?"

"No," she said, once more cracking the whip, eliciting a howl from Del. "They brought me at night in a paneled van with blackout windows. We drove about an hour from Washington, making many stops at lights. There was a lot of traffic noise until we got close to here. They put me in a small bedroom on the second floor."

Tanya pinched his chest again, prompting a loud "ouch" followed by a lingering moan.

"Who are the men?" Del asked.

"Two goons from the Embassy. Dimitri and Georgi. Muscle and errand boys."

"Who's their boss?"

"Colonel Volkov. Everyone works for him."

"A real bastard," Del muttered as Tanya slapped his face again.

"Sorry, but they'll expect to see evidence of my interrogation."

"Can you get a message to Nadia?"

"I'll try, but the Colonel is anxious to know if she's been compromised. I'll have to be careful. What should I tell her?"

Del racked his mind as Tanya cracked her whip. "OWW!" he screamed.

"Tell her you told Volkov that I was a stubborn bastard who gave you a lot of gibberish and general information about the FBI that you already knew, but didn't reveal anything about Nadia that indicates she isn't trustworthy. We need to buy time while my cohorts search for me. Can you prolong the effort?"

"I'll give it my best," she said, slapping Del's cheek again. "But they expect me to get results after all my training."

"Do your best to find out where we are and call Nadia." He provided her secure cell number.

Tanya studied her prisoner. "You need to look well worked over when I leave here," she said. "It has to look authentic, so grit your teeth."

"Do what you have to do," he said as the tip of the whip connected with his left leg and drew blood.

Del's howl of pain was genuine this time.

"Again, I'm sorry to have to do this, but you'll have to shed a little more blood for your country," Tanya said, picking up a razor blade and inflicting a slight cut on his upper chest. Several drops of blood issued.

Del added his verbal histrionics as he watched Tanya, and wondered what next.

"One more thing to insure they're convinced of my thoroughness," she said. "We need to remove your undershorts."

Del blinked. "I can't reach them."

"I know," she said, placing her whip on the table before she knelt before him and began to lower his shorts. "Hmm, impressive," she said. "Nadia mentioned that she thought you were quite a man." She worked the undergarment over his feet and rubbed them against some of the blood drying on his leg and chest. "One more thing," she said, picking up the Butane torch and lighting it.

"Holy moly," Del sighed. "What now?"

"The heated instrument will impress the guards," she said, running her fingers over lingering carbon deposits which she then rubbed on the inside of his thighs. "Muscles," she murmured before standing up inches from his naked body, a movement that prompted a spontaneous reaction as Del stared at her exposed, protruding nipples.

Moving away, she pointed at the cushions. "I'll leave them next to the pole so you'll have a bit of comfort. Pretend you're unconscious when I leave. For now keep moaning like you're really hurting."

"That's easy," he said, staring at the domineering woman.

"How would you grade my performance?" she asked.

Del's eyes traveled over the scantily clad woman with the provocative cutouts, and couldn't repress an involuntary stimulation from the eroticism of the scene.

"Oh my," she said, glancing at him. "Nadia appears to be right."

Striding to the door, she knocked. "I'm through in here," she informed the guards. "He passed out."

Chapter Thirty-four

WILLIAMSBURG, VA

Special Agent Charlie Maxwell met with Cynthia in a small office borrowed from cooperative colleagues of the James City County Police Department. "Our good friends at the Inn added you to their hors d'oeuvre servers at tonight's reception. Any experience?"

"Waitress in college," Cynthia replied. "The routine should come back like baking a cake."

"They expect about 150 guests, including Walters and several more members of Congress attending a seminar on health care. My two additional Norfolk colleagues will be affording special attention to the ones seemingly most friendly to him. They're a male and female team that should blend right in—Sheila Montgomery and Wendell Black."

"Hey, I met Sheila at In-Service. She's sharp."

"Pretend you don't know her, of course."

Cynthia smiled. "I know the drill, Charlie. Where will you be?"

"Lurking in the bushes," he laughed. "Just call my cell. Prompt response guaranteed."

***

Anna's train arrived in Williamsburg on time, and a waiting cab had her entering the stately Williamsburg Inn in the historic restored Colonial District shortly before six. A liveried bellman carried her small overnight bag to a second-floor suite where Congressman Walters was bidding farewell to a short goateed man in a brown corduroy jacket grasping a small valise.

"Welcome, my dear," he exclaimed, hugging her possessively as he took her bag and handed the bellman a folded bill. "Come see our suite while I tell you what just happened." He led Anna through the antique-filled sitting room into a large bedroom containing a commanding four-poster bed covered with plump pillows. His eyes glinted as they traveled between the bed and Anna who wore dark blue slacks and a white poplin jacket. A frown appeared when he glanced at his watch. "Damn, it's six-fifteen, and the reception begins at seven. Guess this will have to wait until later," he said with a leer.

Anna smiled. "Waiting can enhance eventual enjoyment."

"Definitely," Walters said with a confident smirk.

"You were going to tell me what just happened," Anna queried.

"Oh, yeah," Walters said. "That was my money contact. I exchanged most of my $500 bills for $100's. The others are in my briefcase," he said, pointing to a large brown leather valise sitting on the bed. "He paid a 10% premium. Bet he got 20%, but that's business, and Quentin's a business-man."

"Quentin?"

"Yeah, but you don't need to know anything more about him. That's the way he likes it. Let me have your $500's. I'll get most of them to him. I need a few of them for tonight. I'll give you your share later. Meanwhile, do you need to change?"

"Yes," she said, handing Walters an envelope containing several of the marked bills. "And, I'd like to take a shower. I feel a little grimy after that train ride."

"By all means, my dear. I need to assemble some packages for later. It's payday," he said as Anna picked up her bag and headed for the bathroom.

Oh, Del, she sighed, slipping out of her clothes. I need you, honey. I pray you are safe, wherever you are.

TYSONS CORNER

Nadia's call to Kevin Ryan spurred a Christmas-like euphoria. "We found Del!" he enthused to Dutton. "Sort of."

"What do you mean sort of?"

"He's alive, within about a hundred miles."

"Please elaborate."

"Nadia got a call from a woman she was trained with a couple of years ago. She was forced to become a torturer, and was with Del just hours ago."

"That's good news?"

Ryan chuckled. "Doesn't sound like it, I agree, but the woman wants to get out, and put on a torture sham in the cellar of a big old home. She's depending on Del to help her defect."

"The guy's a wonder," Dutton said, shaking his head. "Where's the big old house, and do we have a rescue party on the way?"

"That's the problem, boss. We don't know where it is—only that it's about an hour away from D.C. Could be Washington, Maryland, or Virginia. The woman was transported there in a blacked-out van after dark. She's somewhat of a prisoner too, but it's clear she was dispatched by the Russian Embassy, specifically by our old friend, Colonel Volkov."

"So, the good news is that Del's alive, but we don't know where he is. No GPS or cell phone connection."

Ryan nodded.

Dutton picked up his phone. "I'll inform Wayne Jackson at Headquarters. Get the word out to all our troops. And, say a prayer, Kevin. We need all the help we can get."

WILLIAMSBURG, VA

The reception in the glittering ballroom of the restored area's premier hotel was in full swing. Congressmen and women, along with effusive aides, mixed gaily with affable lobbyists. Cocktails flowed freely, and trays of appetizing hors d'oeuvres', loaded with regional seafood delicacies, were presented by uniformed servers that included Special Agent Cynthia Chalmers. Soft music flowed from overhead speakers. The volume of conversation escalated as libation consumption increased.

Centered prominently in a group of attentive associates was Congressman Jason Walters, nattily dressed in a grey Brooks Brothers suit, standing proprietarily aside Anna, resplendent in a white silk sheath with jade embroidery that subtly defined her curvaceous figure. Diamond earrings sparkled from her delicate ear lobes and were reflected in her dark eyes. With a lock of waist-length, jet-black hair trailing over one shoulder, the striking woman of exotic American-Chinese heritage prompted numerous admiring glances.

"Isn't she beautiful?" Walters whispered to a hovering colleague. "And she's mine for the night," he added with smug conviction.

"Lucky guy," his companion agreed, selecting another crab-stuffed mushroom from a passing server.

Enjoy, Cynthia thought, trying to catch snatches of their conversation.

The male and female agents from Norfolk circulated comfortably around the room, carefully observing the legislators huddling close to Walters. A list of attendees supplied by the Inn manager helped identify two of particular interest, a tall, gaunt Representative from New York, and a plump bleached–blonde from Minnesota wearing a too-tight red dress.

"What a night!" Walters declared loudly to his group. "We all win!"

We'll see, was Anna's thought.

Chapter Thirty-five

SOMEWHERE

Del was dozing on the cushions a few hours after Tanya left when the ceiling light flashed on. The sound of the dead bolt was emphatic before the door opened and the same two men walked in, one carrying a tray that he placed on the table. "Dinner time," he announced. He then pulled a pistol from his pocket and trained it on Del as the other man approached to unlock one of the cuffs and release him from the metal pole.

"Do you have to keep these on?" Del asked. "I'm not going anywhere, and I need to go to the bathroom."

The guards looked at each other and exchanged words that sounded Russian. One shrugged, and the other proceeded to remove both cuffs. "Don't pull anything," he grunted, slipping the cuffs into his pocket.

"Eat," the second one ordered, pushing Del to the solitary chair.

"Can I put my shorts back on?" Del asked.

The pair looked at each other again. "Okay," the taller one said, tossing the blood-stained garment to Del.

"Thanks," Del said, slipping them on. "That might help the Judge be lenient when he sentences you."

A derisive snort emanated from beneath the hood of the second man. "Tanya will beat the jokes out of this clown. Enjoy your meal," he added. "It might be your last one."

Both left following the ominous words, and the dead bolt slammed home outside the formidable door. Del hoped the food would be more elevating.

Looks and smells like goulash, he thought, removing the paper towel covering a tin bowl.

Two slices of brown bread were on the tray, along with another carton of milk. Same dairy, expiration date a week from when he was abducted, indicating they did some recent shopping, Del concluded.

Pretty tasty, he decided, using the only utensil provided, a small plastic spoon. How can I use it as a weapon or means of escape? And the metal bowl? His imagination was spinning, leaving him with the feeling of running in place.

While hurrying to finish the food before it cooled, Del's mind raced in search of ways of extracting himself from his plight. Recollections of previous perilous situations flashed through his memory, especially his escape from a wine cellar in the Sierra Nevada Mountains. Also, his recent deliverance from imminent murder at the hands of a psychotic killer in San Francisco. That brought an immediate mental picture of his beloved fiancée who had faced death with him there, and who was currently dealing with a corrupt legislator. Sure hope you're doing better than me, honey. Now, what can I do with the bowl and plastic spoon?

Mind swirling, Del studied the old, dented pot, focusing on its single elongated, horseshoe-shaped handle of approximately three inches width. His eyes dwelt on the screws that attached it to the pot, one of which appeared to be slightly loose. With his hands now free of the handcuffs, his fingers went to work.

Ten minutes later, with the assistance of the plastic spoon and two broken fingernails, he had succeeded in removing the loose screw. Elation tanked, however, when the second screw refused to budge.

His eyes scanned the room and settled on the folding cot. Moving there with the pot, he examined its possible use and felt his spirits again surge when he felt a sharp edge of a metal bracket connecting the wooden framework of the cot. Would its sharp point fit into the screw head slot? With renewed hope and vigor, Del's hands went back to work.

WILLIAMSBURG, VA

As the reception wound down, Walters turned to Anna. "One more important item before the grand finale," he said, displaying a meaningful gleam in his eyes.

"And what that might be?" she asked.

"We're going to visit Bill and Mildred at their resort. They insist on showing it to us," he said, nodding to his fawning colleagues. "We also have some unfinished business to complete."

Both legislators smiled.

"Whatever you say, Jason. I'm with you," Anna replied.

You can bet on that, Walters mused.

"I need to get my briefcase from the room safe," Walters continued. "Meet me at the front entrance in fifteen minutes," he said leaving the group.

"You'll love our accommodations," Mildred told Anna. "Not as historic as this place, but really plush—fitting for a duly elected Representative of the people."

The smugness of her smile tempted Anna to strangle her on the spot.

Twenty minutes later, Walters and Anna were in his black Buick, headed for the Kingsmill Resort and Spa adjacent to Busch Gardens. Her glance at the speedometer revealed the car substantially exceeding the posted speed limits on the short drive. "Are we going too fast on these narrow roads?" Anna queried as the car careened around a sharp curve.

"I don't like to waste time," Walters replied, "and don't worry about these yokel cops. I'm a United States Congressman!"

Within fifteen minutes they were on the grounds of the sprawling resort located along the James River, and being welcomed by Walters' New York colleague in his posh suite. The bleached-blonde member of Congress from Minnesota was already there, holding a large glass of bourbon. "Nifty, isn't it?" she said. "I've got one just as fancy next door. Makes one work all the harder for our constituents," she laughed before taking a large gulp. Her eyes roamed to the large briefcase in Walters' grip, her head nodded, and a pleased smile emerged.

Walters proceeded to the well-stocked bar and filled a cocktail glass with Chivas Regal scotch. "To next week's victory," he toasted. "And what may I get for you, Anna?"

"Just a little white wine will do. I've already had more than I usually drink."

"There's a lot more," Walters exclaimed, taking a generous sip. "Don't be bashful. Our celebration has just begun."

"Let me show you the game room," the New York legislator said to Walters with a wink and a glance at the briefcase, "while the ladies exchange recipes."

As soon as the men disappeared into the bedroom, Mildred sidled close to Anna. "Having fun with Jason?"

"He's quite entertaining," Anna replied evasively.

"You know what I mean," the woman persisted, taking another large swallow from her glass. "Are you satisfying him?"

Anna paused before replying. "I'm not comfortable discussing personal matters," she finally said.

Mildred from Minnesota sipped more bourbon and released a small smile. "Well, just so you know, women can often provide much more enjoyment, and you're a very attractive woman who looks like she could make beautiful music with an affectionate friend. Call me sometime."

Good Lord, Anna was thinking when the men returned to the sitting room. She watched Walters refill his glass before beckoning to Mildred, who also mixed another drink before following him into the bedroom.

"Great seminar," the New York Congressman said to Anna with a satisfied grin on his way to the bar. "Are you enjoying yourself?"

"It has been very interesting," Anna replied, beginning to feel uncomfortable about the way the man's eyes roamed over her body.

"You help make it interesting," he said, moving closer. "You had all the men drooling at the reception. Do you always have this impact?"

"I…I don't know, Bill. I'm just me."

"Well, just me is plenty, so if old Jason doesn't treat you right, don't hesitate to let your New York friend help out."

What a pit of vipers, Anna was thinking when the bedroom door opened and Walters and Mildred emerged. He carried his old leather briefcase like it was empty. Payoff time, Anna surmised, trying to mentally record the evening's events for future use, and visualizing the treated bills in the grubby hands of Walters' colleagues.

"One for the road to memorialize a rewarding day!" Walters shouted.

"Hear, hear!" Bill from New York agreed.

The three legislators resumed their assault on the taxpayer-funded liquor supply. Anna slowly sipped her wine.

When an ornate clock chimed eleven, Walters placed his nearly empty glass on the cocktail table and looked at Anna. "We have some unfinished business to attend to back at the Inn." His words sounded slurred, his intentions obvious. "Are you ready?" he asked, rising unsteadily to his feet.

"I'm ready," Anna responded with a forced smile that obscured concerns about how she would defeat his plans. *I'm running out of excuses.*

Walters eyed the nearly empty Chivas Regal bottle. "No sense in wasting this," he said, picking it up. "Might get thirsty on the way home."

Within minutes they were speeding out of the resort complex.

Chapter Thirty-six

SOMEWHERE

Del's fingertips were raw from his efforts to dislodge the remaining screw from the metal pot. Stubborn little bastard, he thought, striving to force the sharp edge of the cot bracket into the head slot of the tiny screw. But I'm a stubborn bastard too, he laughed internally, continuing the challenge. Have to do it before the goons return, he was reminding himself when he felt slight movement. Intensifying his efforts, he was further elated to see the screw slowly move. Bully! he felt like shouting as the emerging fastener became more visible and his bloody fingers gripped it tenaciously. Suddenly, the handle sprung free of the pot and he stared at it, imagining its possibilities. He wiped the blood from his fingers on his face and shorts. Add a bit of authenticity, he thought as he hurried to return the pot to the table and cover it with the paper towel. He prayed that no one would notice the missing handle.

Debating where to hide the handle while he pondered how to use it, he decided to bury it in the dirt floor near the pole he had been attached to. Might be handcuffed there again, he reasoned as he reclined on the cushions to rest and think.

A half hour later he was roused from his semi-slumber by illumination of the ceiling bulb, followed by a shout from outside. "Back from the door!" was the order from an increasingly familiar voice.

The same two hooded guards entered with drawn pistols, followed by Tanya, garbed in her revealing black leather. Had she renewed the rouge on her nipples, he wondered, or was her appearance overstimulating him?

"Secure him around the pole like before," she ordered, placing her leather satchel on the table. Her whip remained firmly in her grasp.

While the guards reattached Del's hands around the metal stanchion, using what Del believed were his own handcuffs, Tanya pranced around the room like a lion tamer waiting to put her animals through their routines. A sharp crack of her whip signaled her intentions. "This time the truth!" she declared in a throaty voice. The whip cracked again.

Del was impressed by her performance, and strived to display suitable fright that would look genuine to his captors.

"Bring in my special toy," Tanya then directed, waiting while one guard left the room to return a minute later pushing a small wooden cart. Sitting atop the cart was a car-sized battery. Long cables attached to its poles ended with alligator clips. "Guess where these might be attached?" she asked in a mocking tone.

Del tried to increase his expression of fear while watching the guards remove the food tray and head out of the room.

"Yes," Tanya said, cracking her whip once more. "Leave us alone while we play." Her tone was menacing.

As soon as the dead bolt rammed home, she was kneeling on the cushion before Del. "You're going to have to sound even more convincing this time," Tanya whispered. "They're questioning my interrogation skills. We need to give them something to satisfy them," she added, cracking the whip.

Del yelled like a trapped hyena.

"Moan too," she said.

He did his best.

"Did you talk with Nadia again?" he asked.

"Yes, and she fears they suspect she might defect."

Their muted conversation was periodically interrupted with whip cracks and appropriate cries of pain.

"Do you know where we are yet?"

"No. I feel like a prisoner too."

"Do you hear any outside noises?"

"Birds chirping, and a distant church bell ringing once a day around dark. It's pretty quiet except for the planes."

"Planes?"

"Yes, I hear an almost constant drone of airplanes, except late at night when they mainly stop. That has to be close to midnight."

Del's attention soared. "That's very relevant, Tanya. Could be a landing guide path. Have Nadia pass that on to Kevin Ryan. It could pinpoint where we are."

"I never thought of that, Del. You might be smarter than they credit you for."

Del managed a laugh. "Desperate might be more apt. We can't overlook any possible clue. Also, have Nadia tell Kevin that they serve me milk in cartons labeled Blue Moon Dairy. No address listed, but it could be local, and they can canvass where its products are distributed. And mention the church bell—sounds like a call for evening vespers. Might be close. This is all very helpful, Tanya. Keep noting such things and we'll get out of this snake pit. We should make you a deputy FBI agent."

"I think I'd like that," she said, stroking his cheek.

"Who else is in the house?" Del asked.

"Just the two guards and the babushka."

"Babushka? I thought that was a head scarf."

Tanya laughed lightly. "Russian grandmother. She does the cooking and cleaning. Limited English."

"So you know, I broke a handle off the dinner pot. Hope to use it as a tool or weapon. Can you leave me anything from your satchel?"

Tanya paused in thought. "They might not miss a small set of pliers. They check my bag after every visit with you."

Throughout their murmured exchange, Tanya continued the dramatic use of her whip, while Del plied his histrionic skills with resounding yells, whelps, moans and groans.

"What do the guards do all day?"

"Read, sleep, watch porn movies, and try to make me."

Del smiled at the exotic woman. "Hard to blame them. You are quite appealing. How do you avoid their moves?"

"Keep my bedroom door locked, and a sharp knife handy. They tend to respect my reputation. And they fear the Colonel."

"What have you heard from him?" Del asked.

"Loud and clear that he wants to know Nadia's degree of commitment. I believe he plans to kill her if he finds out she's disloyal. He's noted for terminating his adversaries in dramatic fashion as a warning to others. He's a mean bastard. Old KGB."

Del nodded. "I heard what he did to Nadia."

Tanya nodded in return. "He takes what he wants, often viciously. I know."

"We need to get her out of his clutches," Del said.

"Yes," Tanya agreed, shifting on the cushion, exposing a substantial amount of her lower torso.

"I wish you wouldn't do that," Del said, sensing the front of his shorts expanding. "I'm convinced you're a natural blonde."

Tanya noticed the arousal and smiled. "Nadia said you react vigorously."

Del tried to redirect his attention. "Call her again on the number I gave you and report what we discussed. Tell her to let Kevin know we think she's in grave jeopardy."

"Will do," Tanya replied, slapping his face, prompting a lusty scream from Del.

"I need to convince them that I'm employing every technique to make you talk," Tanya said with a gleam in her blue eyes. "I mentioned at the outset in the presence of the guards that I could secure the desired information with either pain or pleasure. I've been trained in both disciplines."

Del pondered her words. "What are you saying?"

"Just speculating," she said, patting his protrusion. "But," she continued, "I believe we need to continue this charade on its present course, so we'll keep the other option on hold." With that, Tanya reached beneath the sparse material covering her crotch area and extracted two small items.

Del's eyes expanded.

"Bacon," Tanya said with a smile. "We're going to fry it." Rising, and again brushing her breasts close to Del's face, she attached one alligator clip from the battery to a piece of bacon she had placed on the table. She then touched the other cable to the opposite battery pole and watched the bacon smoke and sizzle. The strong aroma of burning meat filled the room.

Del screamed, over and over. Loudly.

Tanya followed the same procedure with the other bacon piece, with the same result and Del's lusty accompaniment.

"Oh! Oh! Oh!" he pleaded, "please stop!"

"Well done," Tanya said, pausing briefly for the bacon to cool before returning to Del where she tucked the scorched meat in his shorts. "Tough job, but someone has to do it," she said, giving him a squeeze.

Both stunned and stimulated, Del fought to stifle a laugh. "You're a special case, Tanya."

"To be continued," she said, drawing a small set of pliers from her satchel and pushing them under his cushion. "Good luck," she said, gently caressing his face. "I hope we both survive this nightmare."

Tanya then called loudly to the guards, "I'm through with this pussy. He passed out again."

Chapter Thirty-seven

WILLIAMSBURG

Walters' black Buick was weaving erratically on State Route 199 at high speed.

"Shouldn't we slow down?" Anna suggested in a concerned voice.

"Why? We have things to do," the Congressman slurred, reaching past the Chivas Regal bottle sitting in the center console to pat Anna's knee. The action caused him to jerk the steering wheel and veer briefly over the road's center line.

"We need to arrive safely, Jason, to be able to do anything."

"Not to worry," he was saying when flashing blue and red lights reflected in his rear-view mirrors, accompanied by a wailing siren.

"Shit!" he exclaimed. "Just what we needed."

Wonderful, Anna said to herself.

"This won't take long," Walters assured Anna as he pulled onto the right shoulder of the road. "As soon as they know who I am, we'll be on our way."

Walters lowered his window and waited while a tall uniformed officer approached on the driver's side. "Good evening," Walters said in his most convincing tone.

"Good evening, sir. May I see your driver's license and vehicle registration please."

"What's this all about, officer? I am just driving home."

"License and registration, please, and I must advise you this is being recorded."

"I'm sure this can be resolved," Walters said fumbling to remove his license from his wallet.

"What's this, sir?" the officer said, videotaping the $100 bill Walters held alongside his license.

"It's a $100 bill, sonny. Yankee money. Not some Confederate funny money." His friendly tone had faded.

A second patrol car was heard arriving behind the first unit, delivering a second officer.

"I must ask you to step out of your vehicle, sir," the first officer said.

"What a lot of bullshit," Walters yelled with increasing belligerence. "Don't you know who I am?"

"Your license says Jason Walters."

"That's right, buddy. Congressman Jason Walters!"

"You still need to exit the car, sir."

"Why? What do you claim I was doing?"

"Driving erratically, exceeding posted speed limits by over twenty miles per hour, and going through a red light. You almost struck another vehicle."

"What the hell!" Walters bellowed. "You're harassing me, you black bastard. How did you get on the force? I'll have your badge. Your Governor's a personal friend of mine. I was recently with him at a political rally."

"Please do what he says," Anna was heard to urge from her seat.

"You still have to get out of the car, Congressman, or be removed forcibly."

"You'll regret this, whatever your name is," Walters shouted as he staggered out of the car.

"Name's Hawkins," the officer said. "Ernest Hawkins. It will be on the citation. And what is in that bottle, sir?"

"Scotch. What the hell you think it is. Lemonade?"

"We have an open-container law in Virginia, sir. That's another violation. Would you walk down that white line for me?"

"Hell no! I'm not walking anywhere for you."

"Will you take a breathalyzer test?"

"No way in hell, buster. I know my rights. You can take that gizmo and shove it up your black ass."

The second officer, wearing sergeant's stripes on his neat uniform, watched attentively from the background, silently applauding the professionalism of his rookie patrol officer.

"You are being placed under arrest," Hawkins announced, producing his handcuffs.

"In a pig's eye," Walters yelled, swinging at the officer, missing his target, and falling to the ground near the puddled remains of an overnight thundershower.

Two minutes later, Walters was handcuffed in the back seat of a James City County Police Department cruiser, en route to the Municipal Building Jail. The sergeant, whose nameplate read Wilkinson, approached Anna. "Sorry for the scene, ma'am. He'll be booked and placed in the holding tank overnight."

Anna sighed. I'm not sorry, she wanted to say.

"We need to impound his car. I'll be happy to drive you to the Inn," the officer said.

"You know where we're staying?"

Wilkinson smiled. "Charlie Maxwell is a respected colleague. And, his associate, Cynthia Chalmers, is waiting to welcome you."

Anna's smile of relief was hard to repress.

TYSONS CORNER

Kevin Ryan listened with satisfaction to the report from Charlie Maxwell calling from Williamsburg. "She dodged another bullet," Ryan said. "I'm beginning to believe she's luckier than her fiancée. You know we have a missing agent, don't you?"

"Oh, yeah. I definitely heard that, and hope we're going all out to find him."

"No question, but the search is frustrating as hell. We know he's alive, and in a cellar somewhere, but no idea where. The only good news is the guy's fabulous luck and ingenuity. But, back to Anna. What next?"

"Walters will be in the drunk tank until late tomorrow morning at the earliest. We learned he scored a .12 on the drunk meter—more than legally drunk. There are also a slew of additional charges. His administrative aide is en route to bail him out."

"How about his close friend, the Governor?"

Maxwell laughed. "They had a hard time reaching his office. Political solidarity is a transitory quality it seems."

"How about Anna?" Ryan asked.

"Relieved, obviously. She's driving back in the morning with Cynthia. We'll concoct a plausible story for why she didn't wait for Walters' release."

"And, the center ring for this whole circus—the payoffs?"

"Looks tight, Kevin. We have witnesses to the whole chain of events. The tainted bills are moving through the system. Anna feels certain some of them were in the payoffs to Walters' two colleagues. We identified Walters' local man—Quentin Baxter. He operates a small shop at the Pottery Factory. Known for shady deals. Had a fraud conviction a few years ago and spent some time in the pen. He doesn't want to go back. Should be easy to squeeze. There's a lot of circumstantial evidence, but it looks to me like we have a strong case. I'd say it's time for a celebratory beverage. I'll be having Southern Comfort. How about you?"

"Maalox," Ryan said. "We don't have the glamorous life of you guys in the field."

"*Otvali,*" Maxwell said. "That's a word I found in the Russian-English dictionary when I heard you were bringing your doubled-barreled Russian spy and corrupt congressmen roadshow to our territory. Translated, it means, pardon the crudity, fuck off."

Chapter Thirty-eight

SOMEWHERE

It was growing dark outside when the ceiling light blinked on and the familiar sound of the sliding dead bolt roused Del from his uncomfortable slumber. He carefully scrutinized the same two men for signs they were aware of the missing handle, relieved when one of them placed a tray on the table without comment. Projecting his most pitiful persona, Del asked them to again remove his cuffs, and was encouraged to see them comply. The tall one glanced at Del's shorts and sniffed before they both quickly departed.

Moving to the table, Del found a dinner plate covered with a combination of noodles, sausage, cheese, and peppers. The usual brown bread was replaced with a roll, plus an apple, and another carton of milk. He noticed it had the same expiration date. No address or phone number, which he realized wouldn't help much since he didn't have a phone. He dug into the food that was spicy but tasty. Thanks, babushka, he thought, and please don't try to use the old metal pot.

As soon as he finished eating he located the pliers Tanya had concealed and dug up the pot handle, pondering what he could fashion—a stiletto?, handcuff key?, what? Examination of the inside hardware of the door lock revealed no apparent points of attack. He rubbed his chin in thought, feeling the roughness of a two-day growth of beard, then studied the dirt and dried blood on his palm. You must look like hell, he concluded, returning to his task.

WILLIAMSBURG

Anna and Cynthia enjoyed a restful sleep at the Williamsburg Inn. Cynthia insisted that Anna use the luxurious four-poster in the bedroom, while she slept on a pull-out bed in the sitting room. "You can tell Jason how lonely it was without him."

Both women were giggling like teen-agers the following morning when a call arrived from Walters. "They're making a big deal out of this," he complained, "and they're giving my aide all kind of crap about releasing me. And the damned Governor can't be reached. This never would have happened back home."

"I feel so sorry for you, Jason," Anna managed to say, fighting to sound serious.

Walters continued in an irritated tone. "It might be this afternoon before I get out, and then I have to recover my car. Can you imagine the trouble these hicks have caused?"

"They do seem pretty strict around here, Jason. The hotel people said we had to be out of our room by eleven."

"Maybe you can wait around and ride back to Washington with me."

"Oh," Anna replied, employing the rehearsed story, "while I was talking with a desk clerk about Amtrak train schedules, a nice lady overheard our conversation and said she was driving back to Washington and offered me a ride. We leave in thirty minutes."

"Damn, our special time together has sure gone down the drain," Walters moaned in a doleful tone.

"Yes, it has been disappointing," Anna agreed.

"Well, as you know, we still have some important business to conduct, Anna, in addition to our personal interests. I'll call you as soon as I get out of this hell hole."

"I'll be waiting, Jason."

TYSONS CORNER

Kevin Ryan and Andy Dutton were in Dutton's office analyzing their two major concerns. "Things apparently went well in Williamsburg," Dutton remarked. "Be sure to thank Norfolk for their excellent work there. Their local agent came through with his contacts."

"Norfolk is noted for its quality work, they'll remind you in a second," Ryan said.

"Their motto is 'Small but powerful.'"

"Well they lived up to it," Dutton commented. "That phase of operations seems to be on track. It looks like we're close to putting the final nail in Walters' coffin. It's not easy to make a case with so much circumstantial evidence, but legal counsel believes we have all the necessary elements of fraud, bribery, and money laundering."

"Yeah, white collar crime is certainly more complicated than catching a bank robber in the act."

"You have that right, Kevin. It takes a lot of finesse. Apparently Anna excelled in her role."

"She's a winner, despite worrying about Del."

"What's the latest there?" Dutton asked.

"Hopeful news from Nadia. She was called by Tanya who passed on some potentially great clues—airplanes and a church bell."

"Please elaborate, Kevin."

"Tanya reported hearing a church bell ringing each night about dusk. It sounded fairly close. And a lot of airplane noise—sounds like an airport approach path."

"That should narrow it a lot," Dutton said, adding an afterthought. "I've got one near my residence for planes coming in from the northwest headed for Reagan International. They somewhat follow the course of the Potomac River. They're quieter late at night when there's a noise restriction."

"I would guess there's the same restrictions for planes coming into Reagan from the south," Ryan noted.

"Could be significant," Dutton told his assistant. "Push hard on that angle, and find out what nearby churches ring their bells at vespers. Also expedite the canvass on the Blue Moon Dairy distribution. I'm getting a good feeling that we're getting close to our boy. Wonder how he's doing?"

SOMEWHERE

Del smiled at the device he was fashioning, hoping that one end might work as a crude handcuff key. Bring mine back, boys, was his wish.

Using his new tool, and the pliers Tanya had provided, he managed to unscrew the sharp-edged bracket from the cot. Now I have a blade! He began humming *Happy Days Are Here Again.*

Fearing his weapons might be discovered, he concealed the new blade beneath the porta potty while he deliberated how to use it. Come on inspiration, I need you.

WASHINGTON, D.C.

"Anna! I just got home," Jason Walters announced in his early evening cell phone call. "I'd like to see you as soon as possible."

"Oh, Jason. I'm so glad you're back. I've been worrying about you, and thinking about the horrible ordeal you've been going through."

"Yeah, it was the pits. Those damned rednecks will be sorry when any legislation comes up that they want. And it will be a sorry day when I help that Governor who couldn't be found. Can you come over? We need to take care of business and pursue other matters."

"Gee, I'd love to, but I'm kind of stuck here, if you know what I mean."

"That insurance salesman around?"

Wish he was, Anna thought, visualizing her missing fiancé.

"He's a bit upset about my recent absence, Jason, and I need to comfort him."

"How about me?" Walters demanded.

"I know," Anna sighed. "It's been such a disappointment. Can we handle our business over the phone?"

"Hell no!" Walters almost shouted. "You know what we planned."

Anna tried to sound consoling. "You're not the only one frustrated, Jason. But a day or so will make it even more memorable."

"Yeah, great," he growled. "I'll be busy as hell for the next few days. We vote on the health care bill Tuesday."

Chapter Thirty-nine

Kevin Ryan rushed into Andy Dutton's office. "We have a possible crisis, boss. Nadia just called and said she'd been ordered by Colonel Volkov to leave her job at the South Korean Embassy and hop in a cab waiting for her out front. He told her he had some important information about Del."

"Damn, we should have pulled her out sooner," Dutton grumbled. "How soon is she supposed to leave?"

"Fifteen minutes from the time Volkov called—twelve minutes ago."

"Do we have surveillance units on the way? A tail might lead us to Del."

"Curt Oswald and a second unit are on the way, but they're at least twenty minutes out. Curt was planning to cover her travel home at her normal quitting time."

"Double damn, Kevin. With what Tanya reported earlier, it looks like they may have figured out that Nadia is defecting. Hope it wasn't anything learned from Del."

"No way I could believe that, Andy, especially from what Nadia reported about Tanya's sham interrogations."

"I agree, Kevin. And that brings up another important issue—our promises to her to get her grandparents out of Russia. If the Russkies are on to Nadia ,we have to activate the plan there. Call the Agency and tell them it's a go."

"Will do."

"What do we hear from Oswald?"

"He's racing towards the Embassy."

WASHINGTON, D.C.

Nadia recognized the driver of the familiar cab idling outside the embassy on Massachusetts Avenue and slid into the back seat. Viktor Markov drove swiftly away.

"Good afternoon, Nadia," Colonel Serge Volkov greeted in a somber tone from his side of the rear seat. "It is good to see you again."

Nadia felt a cold chill. "Good afternoon, Colonel. You said this was urgent, and that you had some important information."

"Yes, about your martial arts partner. Remember him?"

"Yes, I haven't seen him lately."

"You know he's an FBI Agent?"

"Certainly. We all know that. I reported it."

"A dumbbell, you said, who didn't know who you worked for."

"That's what I reported."

"But maybe not so dumb?"

"That's always possible, Colonel."

"Perhaps smart enough to change your loyalty to our homeland?"

"I've always been loyal to our homeland."

"And to your grandparents?"

Nadia felt her heart leap. "I love my grandparents."

"Of course you do. It would be a shame if something happened to them, wouldn't it?"

Lord, Nadia prayed, I hope the FBI's promises come through.

Volkov smirked. "I've come to believe that your loyalty has been compromised. What was it? Money? Love?"

"I don't know what you mean, Colonel. I've always done what was requested of me."

"Yes, you have been good at your art. I know how skilled you can be. Remember?"

"I'll never forget it, Colonel."

Volkov laughed. "Give me your purse."

Nadia handed it to the burly man who searched the contents, extracting her cell phone. "You should be more careful who you call," he said, grasping a set of heavy-duty pliers and crushing the device. "And for anyone trying to find you, adieu," he said, lowering the window and tossing the phone into the path of a lumbering city bus that completed its destruction. "A sample of what happens to traitors," he said, slapping her face. Addressing the driver, he said, "Take us to our special place, Viktor. We will continue our conversation there."

* * *

Special Agent Curt Oswald uttered an uncharacteristic obscenity as he ploughed through heavy late afternoon traffic. The GPS signal he had been tracking had suddenly stopped minutes before. His frantic search amongst a host of cabs was disheartening. Communications with the second FBI unit disclosed similar frustration. He reported the negative results to Kevin Ryan.

TYSONS CORNER

"Sitting and waiting is the pits," Ryan complained to his boss as they awaited word from Nadia.

"We could call her," Dutton said, "but that might interfere with what's going on. It's probably better to wait for her to call us."

"There is a little good news," Ryan said. "The canvassers learned that Blue Moon Dairy is a small one in Loudoun County, and that they service a number of independent convenience stores in Northern Virginia. Agents are checking those stores for any leads on customers—a really long shot since we don't know who they are, only that they may have Russian accents."

"You're right, a really long shot," Dutton agreed. "Anything on the church bells?"

"There are a surprising number of churches with bells in the area, but so far we've learned that not all ring them regularly, and fewer still at vespers. We're working hard on that," Ryan concluded.

* * *

Nadia looked out the cab's tinted windows as it proceeded through Georgetown and over the Key Bridge onto the George Washington Memorial Parkway heading west. "Where are we going?" she asked.

"Somewhere where we can talk and learn the truth," Volkov said. "I don't like to be deceived. And, I know you are skilled in the martial arts, along with your other talents, so hold out your hands." He pulled a set of plastic hand cuffs from his jacket pocket and bound her wrists. "Do you want to tell me the truth now, or do we need special treatment?"

"I still don't know what you're talking about, Colonel," Nadia said, prompting Volkov's scowl and another slap across her face.

"We shall see what loosens your tongue," he said in a menacing tone.

Ten minutes later, after crossing the Washington Beltway and making a series of turns, they were on a lightly traveled country road when Volkov produced a black cloth hood and placed it over her head. "A little extra security," he said, letting his hands slowly slide down her upper body and linger on her breasts. "What a shame to waste such beauty."

* * *

They were soon seated around a large table in a country kitchen of a stately old home.

Pots and pans hung suspended by their handles from overhead racks, except for one old handle less pot that rested on a counter. A heavyset middle-aged woman with bun-tied brown hair and a flower-patterned apron worked in the background while Colonel Serge Volkov presided over the gathering. Sitting to his right was Nadia, her wrists still bound with plastic cuffs, but hood removed. Seated across from her was Tanya, wearing a silk robe with oriental designs. Also seated at the table were Alexei Nikolay and the two guards, Dimitri Malinsky and Georgi Zukof. Bottles of vodka sat on the table, along with glasses and plates of cheeses, bread, and crackers.

"Let us drink to our homeland," Volkov said, filling the glasses. "We all have pledged our loyalty to mother Russia, haven't we?"

Heads nodded and glasses were raised. After draining his glass, Volkov pressed a glass to Nadia's lips, spilling most of its contents on her blouse. "So sorry," he said, rubbing his hands over her breasts. "How clumsy of me." With a leer, he continued. "We are here to resolve if one of us has betrayed the trust placed in us. Sad to say, Nadia is believed to have done just that."

He poured himself another shot of vodka. "Help yourselves," he invited the others. "We have plenty. So, Nadia, would you like to cleanse your conscience in front of your countrymen?"

"I have betrayed no one," Nadia replied defiantly.

"Demonstrate your dedication," Volkov said, pouring everyone another large measure of vodka. He downed his, and watched as the men enthusiastically complied. He smiled as Tanya followed suit, then held another glass to Nadia's lips. She absorbed a few drops before Volkov let the rest run down her front. He picked up a napkin and again rubbed her damp blouse. "Nice," he said to the men. "Don't you agree?"

Three male heads nodded vigorously.

"Maybe Tanya can extract the truth," he said. "Show us your special costume," he directed, focusing everyone's attention to her.

With an almost imperceptible nod to Nadia, Tanya rose and removed her robe, revealing her skimpy garb. The men's eyeballs seemed to swell, along with other organs, as they admired the provocative sight. They all gulped more vodka.

"Down, men," Volkov ordered, his upper lip damp with perspiration. "Colonels have first choice. Perhaps later," he added with a promising wink. He tossed down another vodka shot.

In the background, the cook had remained busy with a large pot of stew that she finally brought to the table. "Eat," she said in heavily accented Russian.

"Have a vodka," Volkov invited. "We are celebrating our glorious homeland."

"*Spaseeba* (Thank you), I don't drink" she said, adding, "I've seen what damage it can do."

"So be it," Volkov said dismissively, imbibing yet another drink. "After this feast we go to visit our special guest."

Chapter Forty

<u>SOMEWHERE</u>

The noise outside the door was louder than usual when the overhead light blinked on. "Away from the door," a slurred male voice demanded, followed by the entry of the taller guard. The second hooded man unsteadily carried a tray with the handle less pot. Del's surprise was acute. An oversight? A message? What the hell? Tanya then appeared, dressed in her same scanty costume, grasped possessively by Colonel Volkov. Finally, and most surprisingly, in the firm grip of Viktor Nikolay, was Nadia, hands bound in front of her.

"Nadia!" Del gasped.

"Hi, Del. It's been a long time."

"Good to see you, but what are you doing here? And cuffed? You're a loyal Russian."

"Cut the bullshit," Volkov interjected. "We know she's a traitor. All we need to find out is how much damage she's done. That's why Tanya is here. She'll be able to uncover her secrets. You've spent some time with her and know her capabilities." His smile was malevolent.

"She's a sadistic bitch!" Del shouted. "A monster," he continued. "She gets off on pain and suffering. What a disgrace to womankind!" He hoped he sounded convincing.

"Thanks for the testimonial," Tanya said, striding over to firmly slap his face. Sorry, she thought.

Forgive me, was Del's mental apology.

Volkov snorted. "It appears you know each other well. Perhaps you can become even better acquainted before you meet your maker."

"Your days are numbered, Volkov," Del said with bravado. "The FBI will have your sorry ass in a vice before you know it."

"Still a smartass," Volkov said, walking over to punch Del in the ribs.

"Free my hands and I'll return the favor, you coward," Del responded, a statement that prompted another punch to his kidneys. "American pig!"

"Russian bastard," Del replied, provoking another blow.

"Enough of this frivolity," Volkov said. "We need you fully alert when you die. And you'll have company," he said, "unless this woman can convince Tanya that she's innocent. You know how much Tanya enjoys her job." He pointed to Viktor. "Bring her here. You've always admired Nadia, now you'll have a chance to get a better view of the object of your desires."

Pulling a switchblade knife from his pocket, Volkov cut the connection linking Nadia's wrists, then dragged her to the second metal pole where he secured her arms around it with another plastic tie.

"Now," he said to Viktor," it's your turn to examine the merchandise. Undress her."

The taxi driver leaped to the challenge, but danced away when Nadia kicked out at him as he approached. He judiciously elected to approach from the rear, and from that position managed to unbutton and remove her blouse. He next succeeded in unzipping and removing her skirt, despite Nadia's vigorous efforts to obstruct his efforts. His arousal was prominent, his eyes feverish with lust.

Despite Nadia's evasive movements, Viktor succeeded in unhooking and removing her bra, then inserted his fingertips inside the elastic waistband of her panty hose. He had lowered the garment about three inches when Volkov shouted "STOP! Let's leave a little mystery. Lovely, isn't she?" he rasped, staring at his tearful semi-nude captive. Ignoring the visibly disappointed cab driver, Volkov walked over to the traumatized woman and lifted one of her bountiful breasts in his hand like he was weighing a ripe melon. "Nice and firm," he declared with a leer.

Nadia spat in his face.

Stunned, Volkov reared back, then backhanded her, drawing a trickle of blood. "*Suka*" (Bitch), he shouted.

"Mudak" (Asshole), Nadia rejoined.

With barely restrained rage, Volkov waved his switchblade perilously close to Nadia's breasts. "Maybe I should remove one of those to remind everyone not to fuck with Colonel Serge Volkov! But, no, to show that I'm a forgiving man, I'll delay punishment for your deplorable act of disrespect." With a swipe of the razor-sharp blade, Volkov cut the plastic connection between Nadia's wrists. "I'll leave this FBI mongrel connected around his pole," Volkov sneered. "This traitor can comfort him while they think about their fate."

Volkov glared. "Tanya will enjoy her visit with you in the morning. For us," he growled, "there's more vodka upstairs. And," he snickered, "Tanya and I need to review her training program."

Tanya's chill equaled Volkov's anticipated thrill.

* * *

Silence reigned after the dead bolt slammed into its receptacle, followed immediately by extinguishment of the ceiling light. Faint illumination filtered through the solitary window as nighttime darkness approached. "Welcome to the palace," Del jested. "Sorry to get you into this jam."

"I'm honored to be with you," Nadia said, "and I know we will manage to survive. What should we do first?"

"First, look around the space so you know where things are before it gets pitch black. Secondly, bring that pot of food over. I'm famished. Then we can discuss our options."

FBI Code Name: SPYTRAP

Chapter Forty-one

TYSONS CORNER

"Good Lord," Dutton moaned. "We've gone from bad to worse. Two of our key people are missing and we don't know where they are. Fine investigators we are!"

Ryan nodded agreement. "I share your frustration, but it's only a matter of time before one of our investigative avenues pays off. I feel it in my bones—the church bells, plane landing paths, dairy. It'll all come together suddenly."

"I like your optimism, Kevin."

"The lull before the storm, boss. I expect us to be overwhelmed with work any minute. We'll be moving on the Walters case soon after the vote is taken tomorrow."

"Things all cleared with the Departmental lawyers? It's a big deal when you charge and arrest members of Congress."

"Hourly conversations, sir. The White House is naturally interested as well. We're dealing with sensitive political interests."

"An understatement, Kevin. I yearn for the old days when politics were far removed from our investigative role."

"Amen," Ryan was agreeing when his cell phone rang. "She's here," the whispered female voice said. "Can't talk now. Will call. Volkov planning to kill both." The click was distinct.

Dutton's eyes were questioning.

"Tanya," Ryan said. "She said 'she's here.' I'm sure she meant Nadia. Said she couldn't talk but would call back. And, she said that Volkov plans to kill both, which I assume means Del and Nadia."

Dutton looked grim. "We need a break, Kevin."

* * *

Anna and Cynthia Chalmers were in Anna's Westin Hotel room, discussing the testimony Anna could provide in the case against the three legislators involved in the health care fraud and money laundering. They reviewed the surreptitiously recorded conversations where Walters boasted of his ability to purchase votes, as well as his statements about laundering money derived from the sale of illegally imported ivory. "Your first-hand witnessing of the transfer of the marked currency will be crucial evidence," Chalmers declared. "You'll be a dynamite witness."

"If only Del was back with me," Anna said wistfully. "I worry about him all the time."

Chalmers patted her friends' hand. "He's a survivor, with a reputation for good luck. He'll be back with us before you know it."

Anna forced a hopeful smile.

TYSONS CORNER

Kevin Ryan hurried into Dutton's office. "Hey, boss, I believe we have that break we've been praying for. An agent on the dairy canvass found a convenience store in Great Falls that may have sold milk and food to Del's captors."

"Details, Kevin."

"A few days ago a middle-aged woman, described as looking like a peasant, and speaking with a heavy accent, bought a bunch of half-pint milk cartons, plus some meats and vegetables. The clerk particularly remembered her because she was asking for things like turnips, beets, and cabbage. They didn't have any, and she directed her to a farmer's market down the road. The woman was accompanied by a tall, dark-haired man in his thirties or forties who didn't say much but exchanged a few words with the woman that sounded Russian. They paid in cash, so no paper receipt."

"That's just a few miles from my place," Dutton said, "and close to the aircraft landing path. Any nearby churches that ring vesper bells?"

"We're concentrating on that. There's a lot of big old homes and estates in that area."

"Like mine," Dutton remarked with a laugh. "What's that movie about the spy next door?"

Ryan chuckled. "Wouldn't that be something?"

"Things are looking up, Kevin. Keep the pressure on."

SOMEWHERE

"Did you have something to eat, Nadia? This is pretty good."

"Yes, I had a bowl of it upstairs."

"Can you tell me anything about where we are?"

Nadia recounted what she recalled from the drive, noting she was blindfolded the last few minutes, and that Volkov had destroyed her cell phone. "How do we escape?" she asked. "I believe Volkov intends to kill us."

"That's what Tanya said."

"She's our secret weapon, Del. Aren't we fortunate?"

"And a wonderful actress," Del said with admiration. "I expected the worst when she strode in with that whip."

"And her costume. Doesn't leave much to the imagination, does it?"

Del grinned. "You Russian ladies seem to burst with beauty."

"Did she arouse you?"

"Am I human?"

"We have both noticed that, but back to our escape. What do we do?"

"If you reach under my cushions you'll find the tool I fashioned from the handle of that pot. It might work as a handcuff key. And, by the way, I'm surprised that the cook didn't notice it missing. What's the story on her?"

"I don't know, maybe Tanya can clarify, but I noticed that Volkov treats her like dirt, and she doesn't look too happy. Now let me search for your tool."

Both laughed at her words as Nadia knelt on the cushion to retrieve the implement. Skin brushed skin. "My," Nadia said, "you feel cold. Found it," she said seconds later, her body brushing his as she stood up.

"I think we are going to experience another challenge," Del muttered. "See if you can insert the tip in the hole and twist."

Nadia giggled. "Sounds like certain instructions."

"I'm going to have to spank you, Nadia, if you don't stop teasing."

"Promise?" she said, striving to work Del's improvised key into the lock, while he attempted to avoid staring at the enticing orbs jiggling before his eyes.

"I think it's in," Nadia said triumphantly, following with a vigorous twist that produced a click and opened the cuff on Del's right wrist.

"All right!" Del exclaimed, extracting his arms from around the pole. "We're on the way."

"What now?" Nadia asked.

"Let me show you where I hid the blade," he said, leading her to the portable toilet where he retrieved the part. He pointed to the crude facility. "Fancy," he said. "Help yourself."

Darkness was rapidly arriving as Del took Nadia's hand to lead her to the cot. "Your feather bed, madam. You sleep here. The blanket is rough, but warm."

"How about you?" she said, rubbing his arm. "You feel awfully cold."

"I'll sleep on my cushions by the pole. They'll expect to find me there when they return."

"But I can feel you shaking."

"I'll survive," Del said. "Now, I need to get over there while I can still see the way. Good night, cell mate. Better days ahead."

"Any prohibition against kissing your cell mate good night? Volkov threatened our time on earth as short."

"I won't let that happen to you, Nadia. You're too precious," he said, moving into her open arms. "It seems like we did something like this before," he gasped.

"And you survived," she responded, moving closer.

Electricity flowed as the bare-topped bodies pressed together. Del felt other bodily urgings fighting for recognition.

Nadia whispered into Del's ear. "This might be our last chance."

Del broke free, groaning. What's the breaking point he asked himself as he thought of Anna and stumbled away.

"Nadia rarely loses," Nadia said into the darkness.

Total darkness soon engulfed the room.

"Are you sleeping?" Nadia asked several minutes later from her cot.

"No, and I don't imagine you're comfortable on that poor excuse for a bed."

"I've enjoyed better. Are you cold?"

"Making do," Del replied. "I'm sandwiched between the two cushions. How about you?"

"The blanket is very much appreciated. I don't have much on."

Del couldn't avoid the visualization. "We'll get you fully dressed soon."

Her reply was muffled.

"Try to rest, Nadia, and think of how to get us out of here. Tomorrow is another day."

"And tonight is tonight," she said before lapsing into silence.

It was an indeterminable and mind-troubling period before Del awoke from his restless slumber. He felt movement next to his cushions. Suddenly alert, he felt a body slipping alongside him, and a blanket thrown over his shoulder. "You won't be of any use to either of us if you freeze to death," a seductive voice whispered. "Our body heat might help us both survive."

Astonished and speechless, Del pondered the merits of their situation.

Chapter Forty-two

TYSONS CORNER

"Who will make the arrests" Dutton asked Kevin Ryan. "The agents who signed the affidavits and conducted most of the background investigations, Abbott and Sullivan, along with Chalmers and Oswald who have been close to the case."

"I'd like to put the cuffs on Walters," Ryan said.

"I know, Kevin. It's a satisfying moment, but those folks have earned the privilege. I'm saving you for another special event."

"I yearn for the field."

"You'll get your chance," Dutton promised. "How is Anna holding up?"

"Like a pro. Still worried about Del, but encouraged that he's alive and close."

"Oh," Dutton said, "I mentioned to Lydia about the church bells. She said she hears them daily, and so would I if I didn't work so late. A little dig about our lovely working hours. Anyway, she estimated the originating church is within a mile or two. The circle compresses."

"Closer to you," Ryan jibed. "You harboring spies?"

"I've been a little suspicious about my dog, Rambo," Dutton laughed before picking up a ringing phone.

SOMEWHERE

First light partially illuminated the cell shared by Nadia and Del. She was back on her cot, huddling under the blanket after she had relocked

Del's hands around his pole. "Another little detail you needed me for," she said, kissing him goodbye.

Del was again compressed between his cushions, his improvised handcuff key back in its place of concealment. They awaited the arrival of their captors which came early.

"Breakfast is served, back from the door," a familiar deep voice announced at the same time the ceiling bulb lit.

Del looked across the room at Nadia, who smiled back as she rubbed her sleepy eyes. She lowered the blanket to her waist and smiled again.

One gun-bearing guard waved his pistol menacingly at the prisoners as the taller one placed the food tray on the table. "One of you sits," he laughed. "Feed the other anyway you can."

Nadia ambled to the table, distracting his attention until she was within reach, whereupon she snatched the hood from his head. "Oh, so handsome," she cooed, studying his features before he hastily recovered his head.

"You shouldn't have done that," the startled man admonished in a heavy accent.

"The Colonel will be angry," his partner warned. "Better not tell him. Let Tanya handle it."

"Okay," the confused man said, hurrying to leave the room with his partner. "She will be along as soon as the Colonel leaves her bed."

* * *

"That could have been dangerous," Del commented when they were alone.

"Aren't we in danger, my friend?"

"You have a point," Del acknowledged. "Eat before the food gets cold."

"Two spoons," Nadia said, digging into the oatmeal.

"The same pot," Del observed. "Surely someone should have noticed the missing handle."

Nadia shook her head. "I don't think the guards are that smart."

"That leaves the cook, Nadia. What's her intent?"

"Maybe Tanya can tell us," she replied, bringing the pot to him. "Need to keep up your strength," she said with twinkling eyes as she began to feed him. "Like a baby," she said, completing the task. "Maybe I should burp you. We need to keep in shape," she added, standing up and beginning a series of limbering up exercises that focused Del's eyes on her movements.

"Have pity on me," Del was pleading when the door opened and Tanya walked in with the guards and her satchel. The taller one pushed the cart with the battery.

Tanya snapped her whip. "Secure her around the same pole," she ordered. "I'll enjoy seeing them dance together. Leave us now, but listen to their cries, and imagine my pleasure." The whip cracked again.

As soon as the guards left, Tanya embraced Nadia. "Your attire looks like mine. Which costume do you thinks excites Del the most? What do you think, Del?"

"I think you're both beautiful, every part of you."

Tanya laughed and cracked her whip. "He's a diplomat, Nadia, even if he looks pretty scruffy. But he screams loudly, which you both need to start doing if those thugs outside are to remain impressed."

Nadia obliged with a full-throated shriek. Del added a loud series of soulful moans.

"So what's the status upstairs?" Del asked, his eyes focused on Tanya's puffed lips. "What happened?"

"The Colonel exercised his seniority. He's nasty when sober. He wasn't sober last night."

"That miserable bastard will pay," Del vowed with a scowl. "Did he disclose his plans?"

"Only that he boasted about having something special in mind for you and Nadia. He left with Viktor after breakfast, but not before Alexei arrived. They both went into the attached garage, and I heard them unloading what sounded like lumber and metal. He then called the guards into the garage and gave them instructions. I tried to enter the garage, but he shooed me away. After he left, I could hear pounding and sawing which went on for about a half hour until the guards came to escort me to you delightful people who need to yell and scream every so often."

Del lustily obliged, followed by Nadia's pitiful cries for mercy.

"We should start a choir," Tanya said, contributing a couple of sharp whip cracks. "I managed to get a short message to the number you gave me—told the man that Nadia was here, and that Volkov intends to kill you both. I couldn't talk long. I should be able to talk longer when the guards are working in the garage."

"How about the babushka? I'm surprised she sent back the pot I removed the handle from. Will she be a problem?"

Tanya shook her head. "I don't think so. She doesn't indicate any love for the Colonel, particularly after he slapped her while complaining about cold coffee."

"A real champion of women," Del said.

"Call Ryan again when you're alone and update him. Tell him we have to make a break soon. When do you think Volkov will return?"

"I heard him tell Alexei he'd see him tomorrow, and that he expected the project completed by then."

"Time is running out, ladies. We need to make our move soon."

Tanya asked, "What should I tell Alexei about today's interrogation? I'm running out of excuses for not producing."

Del stroked his growing beard stubble. "Can you give him some double-talk, and claim you feel Nadia's about to spill her guts with one more session? We need to keep the communication line open."

"I can do that. Now, we need a rousing climax to end this party. Let's hear it!"

"Rousing climax sounds exciting," Nadia said with a grin before unleashing a banshee wail. Del squealed like a stuck pig.

"Good job," Tanya said, squeezing Nadia's bare shoulder. "Slump on the cushions while I call the guards. I'll have them release you from the pole. Hope you don't catch a cold. Do you think you both can survive another night?"

"We'll do our best," Del pledged.

Nadia nodded. "You know how resourceful Russian women are."

Chapter Forty-three

TYSONS CORNER

"The U.S. Attorney has authorized the arrest warrants for the three members of Congress," Ryan was informing Dutton. "The arrests should generate a lot of press coverage."

"Make sure the arresting agents are fully aware of how much scrutiny they will be under, Kevin. They can't make any mistakes."

"They're seasoned investigators, boss. I'm sure they'll perform with complete professionalism. By the way, I just heard from Clarksburg. They identified the fingerprint employee there who disclosed Del's identity—a cousin of the Montgomery P.D. clerk who handled the initial submission of Del's prints. 'A family favor,' she claimed before she was fired."

"Sad," Dutton commented, "how integrity can be so easily squandered. It's another reminder of how vigilant we must be to protect information. We've both seen how much damage can be done when an employee compromises security for whatever justification. Sorry if I sound too philosophical."

"No, I know exactly what you mean. We've had our share of turncoats in the service too. What's the old saying? 'A chain is only as strong as its weakest link?'"

"I've always believed that, Kevin. And, I'm banking on Del to remain a strong link. Wonder how he's doing?"

SOMEWHERE

"We need to set our plan, Nadia. I don't wish to go quietly into the night."

"Nor I, Del. I feel especially anxious to repay the Colonel."

"Let's see what else Tanya can leave behind on her next visit. We have her pliers, the rough blade from the cot, and my crude tool."

Nadia smiled. "Crude?"

Del returned the smile. "We need to stick to business."

"Yes, sir. What else do we need?"

"A club would help. That cot has a lot of wooden parts designed to fold for convenience. Some are about the length of a nice billy club."

"Smart thinking," Nadia complimented.

"Since I'm somewhat tied up at the time," Del scoffed, "you'll have to make the effort. Game?"

"Da," she said, uttering one of the few Russian words Del understood, and began collecting their implements and hurrying to the task. "Typical male chauvinism," she said, "women labor while men luxuriate on plush cushions."

"Sue me," Del laughed, watching Nadia zealously attack the cot.

"Viola!" she proudly announced fifteen minutes later, displaying a piece of wood about fourteen inches long, by two inches wide and thick. "I can get another one from the other end," she said.

"No, that might tip our hosts of what we've done, and could make the cot unusable."

"We still have the cushions," she reminded.

Del changed the subject. "How's your lip?"

"All healed," she replied with sparkling eyes.

"I hate to see you injured, Nadia."

"Battering comes with the territory," she muttered. "I'm more concerned with the fate of my grandparents, and what Volkov might have done to them."

"The Bureau made a promise, Nadia, and I have no doubt it will be kept, regardless of what happens to us."

"That's reassuring, Del, and I'm hopeful that I'll also be able to enjoy the blessings of your great country. Curt took me to the Quantico Marine Memorial where I learned about the sacrifices of your patriotic men and women."

"He's a good guy, and I know he thinks the world of you."

"But I feel so unworthy of him," she said, sitting down next to Del. "You know my past," she added, tears beginning to trickle from her eyes.

"And I know his. He's not one to be judgmental. Don't sell him short, nor yourself. Didn't we agree that the past is past, and what's important is the present?"

"I just want to be free and happy," she sighed, her body beginning to tremble.

Del moved closer. "I'd put my arm around you in comfort if I could, Nadia. Let it out. Tears can be cleansing."

With her bare shoulder pressed against his, Nadia unleashed a torrent of tears before finally falling silent and wiping her eyes. "I feel better," she said. "You're a true friend. Your Anna is very fortunate."

Del rocked against her side. "You're not as tough as you try to appear," he said gently.

"We'll survive, Nadia. We both have much to live for."

"Right," she said, standing up and waving the improvised billy club. "And I know of a skull this club wants to meet."

TYSONS CORNER

Ryan was reporting to Dutton. "Anna called to inform us of her invitation from Walters to meet him tomorrow afternoon after the vote. He told her it was time to celebrate, and then complete their unfinished business. You know what that is."

Dutton smiled. "Won't he be surprised?"

"Tanya also called back," Ryan said. "She said the guards are busy in the garage. Lots of pounding. She managed a peek when they opened the door—said she saw what looked like barrels, and a stack of lumber. She also said it looks like time is running out, and that Del and Nadia feel they have to try an escape."

"Damn, Kevin, why haven't we been able to find them? We know they're so close."

"It's driving me nuts, too, boss. Oh, meant to mention it earlier, but with everything else going on it, it slipped my mind. We found a church that has vespers, and rings its bell. It's an Anglican church on Old Georgetown Pike."

Dutton's head jerked. "I know that church. Drive by it frequently. Tall, impressive steeple. It's within a couple of miles of my place."

"The goal line is close, Andy. I just hope we score before time runs out."

"Well, we won't be bored in the meantime with the fraud arrests going down tomorrow. Get some sleep tonight, Kevin. I sense we won't enjoy that luxury for a while."

SOMEWHERE

Tanya made a brief return visit, with the usual theatrical accompaniments. Left-over stew was delivered, with Nadia serving Del. She remained uncuffed, while Del was again secured around the pole that he began referring to as his wailing pole. With a knowing wink before her departure, Tanya slipped a small file beneath Del's cushions.

"Chance for another treasure hunt," Nadia quipped when the door slammed shut.

"Looks like another frigid night," Del commented.

"But we know how to overcome adversity, don't we?" Nadia said encouragingly.

Chapter Forty-four

WASHINGTON, D.C

The venerable upscale eatery on D Street, a block from the Nation's capital, was alive with buoyant legislators, lobbyists, staffers, and celebrity seekers. Noted as much for its political deals as for its tasty cuisine and generous libations, the *MONOCLE* restaurant was the place to be and to be seen. Multi-million dollar deals were routinely brokered over "working lunches" in the plush surroundings.

Occupying a choice circular table were members of Congress Jason Walters, Mildred Rasmussen, and William Palmer, along with Anna Chen and two young female aides.

Plates of succulent appetizers, including crab imperial, grilled shrimp, calamari, and mini-burgers, shared table space with glasses of beverages that were constantly replenished by attentive waiters. The spirit was celebratory.

"We did it!" Walters crowed, reminding his table mates again of the three-vote passage of the health care legislation they had supported. "Thanks to you two," he pursued, clinking glasses with Rasmussen and Palmer.

He turned to Anna who sat quietly sipping on a gin and tonic. "See what hard work and cooperation can achieve? This is just a sample of what our future can provide."

"You must be very proud, Jason," Anna replied.

"Damn right! It took a lot of arm twisting, and special friends. Let's have another round," he said, signaling a waiter.

Instead of the waiter, a group of six well-dressed people quietly circled the table, led by Cynthia Chalmers displaying her FBI credentials. "Congressman Walters," she announced, "you are under arrest, as are Congressman Palmer and Congresswoman Rasmussen."

"What the hell do you mean?" Walters thundered. "For what?"

"You are all charged with fraud against the government, bribery, money laundering and other crimes, and I advise you this is being recorded. I would also like to advise you of your rights."

"My rights! I know my rights! I'm a U.S. Congressman. I make the laws!"

"Please stand, sir. You are being taken into custody." She produced her handcuffs, as did two fellow agents.

"The same applies to you," Chalmers said, addressing Palmer and Rasmussen.

"This is absurd!" Walters fumed.

"Preposterous!" Palmer added.

"I can't believe this," Rasmussen said with a panicked expression.

"What about her?" Walters shouted, pointing at Anna.

"She has not been charged," Chalmers replied without elaboration.

Walters stared at Anna, his facial expression one of confusion. "What's going on here?" Hints of suspicion flavored his words.

Anna shrugged. "Another disappointment, Jason."

Walters' frown spread as he continued to stare at Anna. "Sonofabitch," he muttered. "I've been set up."

"Now, we'd appreciate your cooperation in leaving with us without creating a disturbance," Chalmers said.

"Where are we going?" the Congresswoman asked.

"The FBI Washington Field Office to start," Chalmers said, "then the D.C Jail."

* * *

"What's going on?" a female tourist at an adjoining table asked her partner as the group moved past.

"Don't know," the man said, "but I'm sure we'll see it on the news."

* * *

His prediction was prescient. TV reporters were waiting outside the restaurant's entrance when the group emerged. Camera lights were shining.

* * *

As the two bewildered Hill staffers remaining at the table jabbered about the stunning events, Curt Oswald approached from a small corner table to address Anna. "May I offer you a ride home?"

TYSONS CORNER

Dutton and Ryan were viewing a video feed from a Bureau surveillance van parked across from the *MONOCLE*'s entrance. "Looks like it went smoothly," Dutton remarked with relief. "Wonder how the media got word?"

Ryan shrugged. "I'm confident it didn't originate with any of our people."

"No, but you can bet we'll be blamed," Dutton remarked in resignation. "Leaks seem to be a common occurrence these days, and with so many people in the Department and U.S. Attorney's office in the know, it's damned near impossible to avoid them."

"It does provide transparency in government, however—right of the people to know and such," Ryan said with a smile.

Their conversation was interrupted with a cell phone call from Chalmers who sounded almost giddy. "Bingo!" she said. "What do you think we discovered in our search of the arrestees?"

"Enlighten," Dutton directed.

"It seems like Christmas morning, sir. Tucked all by itself in a section of Palmer's wallet was one of the special five-hundred-dollar bills. Its serial number matched that of one of the treated ones on our list."

"Bravo, Cynthia. That should nail him."

"But the good news keeps coming," Chalmers continued. "It seems like our targets wanted keepsakes. We found a similar bill in the Congresswoman's purse. Its serial number also matched one on the list. It was inside a plastic bag that also contained a dildo. One's imagination can only ponder where that combination might have come to life."

"You've made our day," Dutton proclaimed. "Congratulations to your whole team, Cynthia. Two down and one to go, and for your information, as we speak, Moretti and Swanson are serving search warrants at Walters' bank to see what's in his strong box. If we find more of the $500 bills from that same source, I believe it clinches our case against him. Do any of them want to talk?"

"We've given them that opportunity. They all want lawyers. Some prominent names were mentioned, but I got the feeling that Congresswoman Rasmussen might want to discuss a deal. Walters and Palmer appear implacable at this point."

"Again, Cynthia, you and your associates have performed admirably. It's always a relief when a major case goes down so well."

"We're all energized here, boss, but remain concerned about Del and Nadia."

"You can be sure we'll be giving that high priority matter our undivided attention now, and we'll be depending on your talents in that pursuit."

Concluding the call from Chalmers, Dutton turned to Ryan. "Pull out all stops, Kevin, and make sure we don't allow little things to slip our minds."

Ryan released a wry smile. "The church bells. You don't forget the details, do you?"

"Try not to, but I recognize we all do from time to time. Call me a fussy old fart."

"I was told you were a hard ass when I was sent here."

"I plead guilty, Kevin. Sounds better than fussy old fart. Just want to make sure we keep each other fully informed of what's going on."

"Why'd you take me as a Supervisor if you had doubts about me when I was assigned here?"

"Never had any doubts, and you weren't just randomly assigned here—I asked for you."

Ryan blinked. "You did?"

"Yes. I checked your background and record of performance, and was impressed. You haven't lessened my confidence."

"That's reassuring."

"I see substantial future advancement for you, Kevin. Hell, I could end up working for you."

Ryan grinned. "With the benefit of your training, I'd probably be a harder ass."

Dutton raised his fist in a gesture of solidarity. "Let's get to work."

Chapter Forty-five

SOMEWHERE

When early morning light began to infiltrate their cellar prison, Del and Nadia assumed their respective sleeping facilities to await the routine arrival of the guards. Some twenty minutes later the overhead light came on, and the familiar door noises sounded. The two hooded guards entered, one brandishing his automatic pistol, the other carrying the food tray.

"Tanya isn't coming today," the taller man said. "The Colonel said he had other plans for her."

"Enjoy your meal," the second guard said, "it might be your last one." With that ominous statement, both men left the room. The door's dead bolt sounded deadly emphatic.

"What do you think the guy's statement about Tanya meant?" Nadia asked.

"Hard to tell," Del replied. "Hope they're not on to her. I believe it's time to execute our plan when the goons return. Ready?"

"Ready and raring," Nadia said, moving to the table and removing the napkin covering the food. "What's this?" she exclaimed, holding up a small piece of paper for Del's viewing. "It's in Russian. Says 'Help me, I help you.'"

"The babushka?" Del speculated.

"Who else?" Nadia asked.

"Maybe that explains the lack of attention to the missing handle. Does she want out too?"

"Could be. A lot of them brought over for menial tasks seek asylum once they see the freedoms here."

"Well, I have no idea how she could help us, but at least it appears she won't be a problem up above. So, when you finish feeding your pretty face, share the wealth and use my crude tool to unlock my cuffs."

"You think I'm still pretty without any makeup on?"

"I think you're still pretty without anything on."

"Oh, the grungy prisoner is thinking naughty again," Nadia teased after devouring a large spoonful of oatmeal. "And he keeps mentioning his crude tool."

"Nadia, I'm going to have you examined by a sex therapist when we get out of here."

"Maybe we can get a group rate," she said with a laugh, bringing the pot to him. "Eat first, or fool around for a while?"

"Please undo me first, so I can throttle your lovely neck."

"There the man goes again, trying to sweet talk the lady."

Del shook his head. "My cell mate's a lunatic."

"But a pretty one, you said."

"Yes, so will my pretty lunatic cell mate please get me unbound?"

Del closed his eyes as Nadia's bare breasts jiggled before his eyes while her hands worked to insert his improvised key into the handcuff lock.

"Oh, damn," she swore. "The tip broke off. What do we do now? You're still locked to the pole."

Del smiled. "Rot here I guess."

"Now who's the lunatic?" she said in a sarcastic tone.

"Did you forget the insurance Tanya left?"

Nadia's face brightened. "The file!"

"Our survival plan. Get to work, it's right below the cushions."

After an enthusiastic search below Del's reclining body, the file was found and Nadia began filing on a connecting link of the handcuffs.

"Tough metal," she muttered as she filed away.

"Keep at it," Del encouraged. "It's our passport to freedom."

Ten minutes later the connection was severed and both rejoiced with a hearty body hug. Del broke the embrace to begin pacing to exercise his legs, like a prizefighter waiting for the fight to begin. "Bring the bastards on," he invited.

TYSONS CORNER

"We have the mobile command van parked in a school parking lot in the center of the steadily diminishing circle," Ryan advised. "It's about a mile from your place."

Dutton nodded. "Almost in my backyard. How ironic. Let's check out the van and see what the troops have been able to come up with."

"Terrific," Ryan exclaimed. "On-the-scene supervision is my baby." Twenty minutes later they were headed northwest in Ryan's Bureau car, and after another twenty minutes in heavy traffic they were seated inside the state-of-the-art FBI mobile command van, being briefed by the senior agent directing the local search. Agents and technicians were busy manning impressive communications equipment crowding the quarters, recording and relaying relevant data.

Cynthia Chalmers and Curt Oswald walked in during the briefing and were welcomed by Dutton who again praised their work in the Walters case. "Glad to have your talent here. This is our winning drive."

"I like your football analogies," Chalmers said. "Love the Cowboys!"

Dutton displayed his Washington Redskins key chain. "We'll see who wins the trophy," he said. "But, I'll still be happy to endorse your transfer to Dallas, after we recover our missing friends."

Chalmers demonstrated her diplomacy. "Let's win this one for Team USA."

"You look like a Dallas Cowboy cheerleader," Dutton said with a grin. "Who does it better?"

"Exactly," Chalmers said, ending their conversation.

Dutton turned to Ryan. "Since we're so close, how about driving me over to my place where I can change into working clothes. Looks like we'll be operating in this vicinity for a while."

Minutes later, as Dutton gazed out the window of Ryan's car at familiar surroundings, he lamented, "It really bugs me that we know our folks are nearby but can't find them."

"We're all frustrated, boss, but they can't be far away."

"You ever have a nagging feeling that something in your memory bank is just struggling to escape?"

"Yeah, I know what you mean."

Dutton scratched his head. "I keep mentally reviewing what Del and Nadia have told us about their surroundings, and what Tanya added—big old house, large country kitchen, dirt cellar floor. Damn," he said, snapping his fingers, "dirt floor. Why didn't that click before? When I renovated our old house several years ago I found a dirt floor in the old root cellar and covered it with concrete. All the original nearby places were built about the same time by the same builder. You've seen the extra-sized lots, and distances the houses are apart from each other. With the hedges and trees, you don't even see them. Our missing friends could be my neighbors!"

Chapter Forty-six

SOMEWHERE

When the usual noontime lunch didn't arrive, the anxiety level of Del and Nadia rose accordingly. "Something's up," was Del's take.

Nadia nodded agreement. "It is unnerving. Help me think of something else. Tell me about your upbringing. I've told you about mine."

"Might put you to sleep," Del joked before summarizing his youthful years, education, and FBI service.

"You took good advantage of your opportunities," Nadia said when he finished.

"Mine were less challenging than yours, Nadia, but you did the best you could under the circumstances, and you're now on the threshold of a new and better life."

"If we survive," she remarked dolefully.

"We will," Del assured with hopeful bluster.

Nadia rose from the table where she had been sitting and began strolling around the cellar. "Need the exercise," she said.

"Ever play blind man's bluff?" Del asked.

"No."

"Good kid's game," Del replied, explaining its rules. "So we don't make too much noise, let's use chirps instead of words. Remember, since we don't have a blindfold, you have to keep your eyes closed," he said, moving away from his pole.

For the next twenty minutes they tried to find each other, using birdlike chirps to signal their location in the dim room. They ended the game in a distant corner with a fervent hug.

"That was fun," Nadia commented. "We had some similar games when I was a child, but never in a cellar."

"And probably not with a guy in dirty Jockey shorts."

"Or with my bare boobs bouncing around."

"It was different," Del agreed.

They embraced again.

"We need to be rescued before it's too late," Del wheezed, breaking free and walking stiffly away.

"You're truly an unusual man," Nadia murmured, moving to her cot. "Think I'll take a rest."

Del returned to his cushions and directed his thoughts to his fiancée. I'm trying my damnedest, Anna.

Their reverie was interrupted about an hour later when the overhead light illuminated. With accompanying sounds outside the entrance door, they hurried to their planned positions. Del extended his wrists around the pole where Nadia made them appear to be still connected. She then retreated to the table and filled the plastic cup with water.

"No food," the taller guard announced upon entry. "We came for you."

To their surprise, both guards were absent their hoods, but not their pistols.

"Nice to see you both in the flesh," Nadia said, "and I'm glad you're here. You can help me with the guy. He's been groaning and acting confused. I was about to take him a cup of water."

The taller guard alternated looks at Del with stares at the topless woman who had bounced to her feet, grasping the water cup. His eyes intently followed her movements as she proceeded to Del's location and hovered above him.

Del groaned loudly as Nadia bent over. "Can you move his head so I can give him some water?" she asked a guard.

As the taller guard began to comply, Nadia threw the water in his eyes and grabbed for his gun. Simultaneously, Del leaped up with unfettered wrists and swung the home-made billy club at the other guard. A shot rang out from the pistol Nadia was trying to wrest from her opponent.

Del's blow to his adversaries' head was severe enough to cause the man to drop his weapon which Del seized. Dazed but still conscious, the guard now stared at the wrong end of his own pistol.

A few feet away, the struggle between Nadia and the second guard raged.

"Damn you, bitch!" the man screamed when Nadia bit his arm, an unsuccessful effort to dislodge his gun which remained firmly in his grip. The overpowering strength of the muscular man eventually overcame Nadia's efforts, and she found herself locked in his grasp, one arm encircling her chest, the other pressing his pistol against her temple. "Drop the gun!" he shouted at Del, "or I kill her."

The man Del had clubbed staggered to his feet and stood stunned as Del trained his own gun on him. "One wrong move and I shoot," Del threatened.

"And I shoot this traitor," Nadia's adversary replied with deadly promise.

The standoff was interrupted with the sudden arrival of Alexei and Colonel Volkov. "What's going on?" Volkov demanded, his eyes scanning the scene.

"These pigs attacked us," the taller guard said in a tremulous voice. "They tried to escape. I should pull the trigger on this woman."

"That might be too lenient," Volkov sneered. "I have something more deserving for her, and this FBI mongrel."

"Bastard," Del said defiantly. "I'll happily shoot this worthless piece of crap."

Volkov stroked his greying goatee. "It's always a treat to contest with this example of American degeneracy."

"I'll take our degeneracy for your abomination any day," Del retorted.

Volkov turned to the man holding his gun to Nadia's head. "On the count of three, shoot her. Then shoot this clumsy clown who let himself be disarmed by the American imbecile. One, two…"

"Wait!" Del yelled. "Don't shoot! This woman is worth more than all of you miserable bums combined. You can have the gun."

"Drop it on the cushion," Volkov ordered, watching intently as Del complied.

"A wise decision," Volkov said, gesturing for the man holding the gun to Nadia's head to lower it. He then approached Nadia and slapped her face. "Traitor," he said with contempt. "Tie her hands, and find her blouse. It's even cooler upstairs. We don't want her to be cold before she dies." His accompanying laugh was malevolent.

"And how did he get loose?" Volkov challenged the guards, moving to examine Del's handcuffs as the now rearmed guard leveled his pistol at their prisoner. "Filed through!" Volkov exclaimed, studying the severed link. "How could this happen? Look around, Alexei. See what you can find."

"Not many places to hide things," Alexei said, beginning his search around the pole where Del had been restrained. Lifting Del's cushions, Alexei immediately announced success. "Look! Pliers, a file, and some weird tool."

Volkov studied the implements, his face clouding with a dark scowl. "Where could he get pliers and a file? Did you check Tanya's satchel as required?" he demanded of the guards.

"Always," the taller guard replied defensively.

"But obviously not thoroughly," Volkov said with disgust. "Tanya has some explaining to do. She's either exceedingly careless, or…? I'll certainly find out. Now, bind the hands of our other guest and bring them both upstairs for their next journey. Or, should I say, their last journey?" His laughter was demonic.

UPSTAIRS

Daylight and fresh air made Del feel lightheaded as he and Nadia were led from their cell prison up a steep wooden stairway to emerge through a door onto the front of a large garage attached to a stately ivy-covered residence. "Inhale the smell of freedom," he called to Nadia, who was being tightly gripped on the arm by Alexei.

"It's wonderful," she replied, drawing in the light westerly breeze.

"I have something to show you," Volkov gloated, pressing a remote control device to open the garage door. "Roll it out," he ordered the guards who hurried to an open-sided trailer dominated by a raft resting on two metal pontoons. Several sets of straps and chains could be seen attached to the surface of the raft. "How do you like my invention?" Volkov challenged. "It will be your transportation to eternity."

Del and Nadia remained mute.

"Renders you speechless, doesn't it?" Volkov said. "Wait until you see how it's used." He pointed to Alexei. "Hitch the trailer to the van, and find something to cover this Yankee's chest. We don't want him to be uncomfortable do we?" His laugh was sardonic. "Hey," he added, "use that souvenir T-shirt you just bought. It'll be appropriate for this decadent capitalist."

Alexei smiled patronizingly. "A nice touch, Colonel," he said heading into the house, to return minutes later with a Walmart bag.

Volkov smirked when Alexei extracted a white T-shirt with a large American flag printed on its front and pulled it over Del's head. "America's pride," he jibed. "Isn't it a custom to bury their heroes under their flag?"

"It's an honor we revere," Del said resolutely.

"Our brave patriot!" Volkov scoffed.

"At least we have a country we can be proud of," Del replied, "and one worth singing about," he said, beginning to sing *I'm a Yankee Doodle Dandy*.

"Enough! Stop singing! You sound as bad as you look," Volkov yelled.

He's a mental case," Alexei declared as Del then began to whistle.

Nadia smiled as Del whistled *Yankee Doodle Dandy.*

Volkov shook his head. "Crazy as a loon. Get Tanya and load them all into the van. We're off!"

Del kept whistling *Yankee Doodle Dandy.* Loudly.

NEARBY

Dutton and Ryan were standing by their car, saying goodbye to Dutton's wife before returning to the command center. The faithful family dog, Rambo, was calmly roving around the yard when he suddenly became agitated and rushed toward the low hedge separating Dutton's property from his neighbors.

"Rambo! Come back!" Dutton shouted, watching his pet disappear through the thicket. He began running after the black Lab, with Ryan racing alongside him.

"He rarely ignores my commands," Dutton said, seeing Rambo continue to run.

"Who lives here?" Ryan asked between gasps of breath.

"A retired doc who's rarely home," Dutton huffed, looking at the tail of his canine that was now darting between a line of towering Cypress pines bordering the next property.

"Who lives there?" Ryan puffed.

"Leased out by a college professor on sabbatical in Europe," Dutton managed to say between labored breaths.

Emerging through the trees, they saw Rambo circling around and sniffing a concrete driveway. In the distance on the entrance road, they saw the rear of a flatbed trailer being towed by a black van.

"Could it be?" Dutton wheezed with an anguished look.

Ryan looked similarly pained. "Could be. Let's look in the house."

Cautiously entering through the unlocked front door, side arms at the ready, Dutton called out, "FBI! Is anyone here?"

Silence reigned as they painstakingly searched the first floor rooms, noting a stack of dirty dishes on a kitchen counter and cooking pots on the stove. Empty vodka bottles filled a trash basket.

Carefully climbing the stairs, they heard light muffled sounds coming from a bedroom off the center hall. With Ryan covering him, Dutton pushed open a partly ajar door to reveal a gagged women tied to a chair.

"FBI," Dutton again announced as he removed the woman's gag. "Who are you?"

"I am Olga," the trembling woman said. "I am cook. I try help."

"Who just left?" Ryan asked.

"The Colonel, three of his men, Tanya, and the two prisoners, a man and a woman."

"Where are they heading?" Dutton asked.

"I don't know, but I heard one mention a park."

Dutton immediately called the command center to report the information, while Ryan untied the woman. "Have all surface units start checking nearby parks and get the Hostage Rescue Team in the air," he directed. "See if they can spot the van and trailer. It will be dark soon."

"They've been on standby," Ryan noted, "and they can scramble fast."

"I hope so," Dutton responded. "You heard the woman mention she heard Volkov say he would rejoice in sending them to their deaths. Let's search the place. I'll take the basement. See what you can find in the house and garage."

Rambo was back at Dutton's side. "Good work, boy," Dutton said, scratching his dog's head. Rambo wagged his tail.

* * *

Fifteen minutes later, Dutton and Ryan reconvened in the country kitchen.

"The cellar, dirt floor and all, was just as described," Dutton reported. "Get the Evidence Response Team here pronto to process the place for evidence."

"Might have something more immediate," Ryan said. "I found this in the living room, next to an empty vodka bottle. It's a brochure of the Northern Virginia Park System and includes a detailed map."

Dutton studied the document. "I see a lot of parks."

"Thirty-two," Ryan responded. "A big search area, but we can narrow it down to the closest ones initially, and since they built a raft, I suggest we start with the ones near water."

"Makes sense, Kevin. The raft with pontoons. Why would they go to so much work if they didn't plan to use it? So, what does that leave?"

They examined the map. "Great Falls and the Regional Park on the Fairfax/Loudon County line look like the best prospects," Dutton observed. "Alert the HRT to concentrate on them," he directed. "We almost had them, Kevin. Damn, almost next door all these days!"

"It's not over, boss, but we're inching closer."

"Like a tortoise," Dutton sighed in exasperation. "Let's join the team at the command center."

Before leaving the prison house, Dutton instructed the cook who was busy cleaning up the kitchen. "A group of FBI people will be here shortly to check the house. They will show you their credentials so you know they are the police." He displayed his. "Give them your full cooperation, and tell them everything you know about the people who were here. Do you understand?"

Olga nodded and beamed. "I help good guys. I want stay."

"You will be rewarded," Dutton concluded as he and Ryan hurried to Ryan's car.

Rambo ran with them, and before they could close the doors he had leaped into the back seat. "What do you think?" Dutton asked Ryan.

"I don't know what the rules say, but he led us to Del."

"My take too, Kevin. Step on it."

As they raced to the command center, Ryan briefly shifted his eyes from the curving road to look at Dutton. "I know you don't like to hear 'oh, it slipped my mind' but I got a call just before the latest ruckus from our IT experts that I think you'd like to hear about."

"Okay, Kevin, don't keep jerking me around about the unintentional oversights. What's the deal?"

"They finally traced the location of the cell phone originating the calls, telling us where Del and Nadia were being held."

"Well, isn't that just jolly," Dutton muttered. "We could have used that information a couple of days ago and avoided all this crap."

"There might be a reason," Ryan said in a placating tone.

"How?"

"Seems the IT war continues at high speed. We break through, they block."

"Clarify for my old-tech mentality, Kevin."

"You know how frustrated we've been not being able to reverse engineer the incoming cell calls to pinpoint their origin."

"Yeah, raising cane with my stomach. Hell, the private sector even has Stingray to help them, and our brain trusts seemed to be stumbling around in circles."

Ryan nodded understanding. "We break through, they place a barrier. The opposition has some bright minds too."

"Granted, but ours are supposed to be brighter. What's the bottom line?"

"Our foreign friends found a way to block identifying the origin of outgoing calls on certain Russian-engineered cell phones."

"And Tanya was using one of them?"

"Correct. It's why we couldn't trace the source of her calls."

"Despite all the towers, and pinging, and all that other scientific stuff? We have some talented enemies, Kevin. We better not forget that."

"Right, but we've finally moved a step ahead technically, and we have our secret weapons, boss."

"Which are?"

"American ingenuity, and common sense."

Dutton grinned. "You're right. Our nutty associate used it with information he conveyed about the planes and church bells. He came through again. Now, let's find him before it's too late."

Chapter Forty-seven

NORTHERN VIRGINIA

"Hurry," Volkov urged his driver. "They close the gate at dusk."

Alexei Nicolay nodded agreement. "I look forward to dispatching these enemies of the state to their just rewards."

"You are a true patriot," Volkov praised. "I see a medal and promotion in order for you."

"They sound serious," Del whispered to Nadia, crammed next to him in the van's second row of seats. The tall guard occupied the right window seat next to Nadia.

"Don't forget our Tae Kwon Do training," she whispered back to Del. "We might need it. You feel warmer," she added.

"Wonder why? You're some hot woman, you know."

"Just not hot enough?" she asked, shimmying closer.

"You ever give up?" he said, spirits momentarily elevated.

"Never to the end. You?"

"You've severely tested my tolerance level, Nadia."

"It's been my supreme challenge, cell mate. I'll never forget it."

"I hope your memory bank is long and full."

"Silence!" the adjacent guard interrupted. "You are not supposed to be talking."

"You better practice talking when the FBI questions you," Del said pugnaciously.

"They don't know who I am," the guard retorted.

"But I do," Del replied. "Rosebud."

"Rosebud?" the puzzled guard asked.

"Yes, or whatever that flower is tattooed on your upper left arm."

After a pause, the guard laughed. "Ah," he said in a menacing tone, "but you will be dead. Don't you have a saying, 'Dead Men Tell No Tales'?"

"That's enough," Volkov ordered from the front seat. "You can discuss your future with the fishes."

* * *

A radio report sounded from the HRT helicopter orbiting the area. "No sighting around Great Falls," was the message. "Heading to other parks near the river."

Transmissions from searching surface units, reporting negative findings, were arriving as Dutton and Ryan reached the mobile command center. Doors of a Bureau SUV opened almost simultaneously, dislodging Special Agents Moretti and Swanson, accompanied by Anna Chen.

Dutton welcomed them all with a broad smile. "Looks like the whole Trappers band is here. Let's strike it up."

They were inside the command center but a few minutes when a radio message arrived from an FBI surface unit: "Loudon County Deputy spotted suspect vehicle on the Algonkian Parkway, apparently headed for the park."

"Ten four," a message came from the HRT helicopter. "Headed that way."

"We are too," Dutton, declared, bounding for the exit.

ALGONKIAN REGIONAL PARK

The 838-acre park abutting the Potomac River near the Loudoun and Fairfax County line had closed its gates to the public, but remained open to occupiers of rental cabins. Having reserved one a week before under an assumed name, the occupants of the caravan had no difficulty in gaining entry and proceeding to the water's-edge boat launching ramp. It was almost dark when the van pulled into the large adjacent parking area.

"Your last stop," Volkov announced to his passengers.

Alexei backed the trailer to the ramp, and the two guards helped unload the raft, leaving its pontoons partially submerged. The craft remained tethered to the trailer by a thick rope.

"Faster," Volkov ordered, and pointed to Nadia. "Get her secured on the raft, then the other traitor. Ladies first," he sneered, "then this FBI idiot. I've removed his restraints so I can deal with him fairly."

"Fairly?" Del scoffed, a remark that generated a sucker punch to his ribs.

"Barbarian," Del retorted.

Within minutes, the wrists of the two women were encased in plastic hand cuffs that were then attached by other plastic ties to ringlets bolted to the raft's wooden surface. An assortment of Russian obscenities were shouted at their captors, and Nadia managed to dispatch a strong kick to the crotch of one guard as she struggled against his rough treatment. A smirking Volkov then addressed his prisoners. "You may wonder why I don't just shoot you. So, I'll tell you. It's because Volkov has a reputation to uphold. <u>No one</u> toys with me without repayment. You three have earned a just penalty. My superiors have praised my methods on behalf of our great homeland, so I especially want these two traitors to have time to reflect on the gravity of their crimes against their country." He looked at Tanya and pointed to her satchel laying on the ground. "We provided this woman with the best equipment, and latest cell phone, and she has betrayed us. Ingrate!"

Volkov paused to study the reaction of his prisoners. "You see the little electric motor? It's to propel this raft, which I personally designed, into the middle of your Potomac River. There, the swift current will carry it towards your Great Falls where you will be smashed on the rocks."

"You're mad, Volkov!" Del shouted.

"And you will soon be dead," Volkov said with a sneering expression on his face, seconds before his eyes were blinded by the headlights of the car that screeched to a halt a few feet away.

When Dutton and Ryan leaped out with drawn guns, Volkov grabbed Del and held him in front as a human shield. His own pistol was pointed at the agents, as were those of Alexei and the two guards. "Seems like we have another Mexican standoff," Volkov greeted. "And we have you out-gunned four to two, plus I have this idiot as a shield."

"Surrender and no one gets hurt," Dutton said, noticing Rambo slowly moving towards Volkov.

"What's that animal?" Volkov demanded.

"My dog," Dutton replied.

"I don't like dogs," Volkov said as Rambo inched closer, growling.

"Get him away," Volkov yelled, kicking at Rambo, who responded by biting Volkov's leg.

Volkov screamed and kicked Rambo in the side, sending him tumbling onto the gravel surface. "Call him off, or I'll shoot the cur," Volkov shouted.

"Here, boy," Dutton called, and the dazed dog hobbled back to his side.

"You won't get away," Dutton continued. "We have overwhelming help minutes away," a statement no sooner uttered than the sound of the motors of the HRT helicopter filled the night air. Headlights of other fast-approaching vehicles were also visible in the near distance.

A brilliant floodlight then illuminated the area, accompanied by a loudspeaker command from the hovering Black Hawk: "FBI! Drop your weapons!"

The next few seconds were chaotic. Volkov began shooting at the helicopter. Del broke free and kicked the Colonel's hand while shouting "Cha-gi!", dislodging Volkov's pistol. Dutton slugged Volkov in the stomach, knocking him to the ground. "That's for Rambo, you sonofabitch!"

Ryan cuffed Volkov. "You're under arrest for espionage, kidnapping, assault on a Federal officer, and other crimes," he announced, adding his Miranda rights.

Cynthia Chalmers and Curt Oswald arrived on the scene, followed a few minutes later by a Bureau car carrying Special Agents Moretti and Swanson, accompanied by Anna, who with streaming tears rushed into Del's welcoming arms.

The two guards promptly surrendered their weapons and were cuffed, one of them claiming ignorance of what was going on. "Stick to your story, buddy," an arresting agent said with a laugh. "I'm sure it will be believed in court, and it will go over big in prison."

The helicopter came to a quick landing nearby, keeping its rotors revolving as the pilot shouted, "Jeff's been hit!"

HRT operators quickly exited the aircraft, supporting the co-pilot who had an emergency bandage wrapped around his right hand. A medical-trained associate began to provide additional treatment as the wounded man rested on the ground.

During the melee, Alexei slipped away, untied the rope to the raft, and pushed the craft into the water. Starting the electric motor, he began quietly moving away from shore.

"They're getting away!" someone shouted, directing all eyes to the slowly disappearing raft.

"Where are they going?" the HRT commander asked, as the group huddled near the helicopter pilot's window.

"Volkov said they were headed for Great Falls, and the rocks there," Del reported. "The women are chained to the raft."

"That's about eight miles by way of the river," the pilot said. "We need to get them off before then."

"How bad is your co-pilot injured?" Dutton asked.

"Right hand wound; bullet came through his open window. Doesn't appear critical, but he's immobilized."

Cynthia Chalmers spoke up. "I used to fly these things for a living." The helo pilot looked quizzical.

"Air Force. Captain. Flew Black Hawks in Iraq. Mucho hours. It's been years, but it's sort of like riding a bike. You never forget."

"I'm Sam Carr," the pilot said, extending his hand. "Welcome aboard."

"Cynthia Chalmers," she said returning the greeting.

"I've had water rescue experience in the SEALS," Ryan announced. "Might be helpful."

"Definitely," the pilot responded. "Hop in."

"You're not going without me," Del declared, grabbing Tanya's abandoned satchel before climbing into the helo.

"That's it," the pilot said, revving his twin engines. "Jeff will be treated here by one of the HRT operators. We need to catch up with the raft."

* * *

Ten minutes later Alexei Nikolay had the raft about to enter the swift-moving center channel of the Potomac River, swollen by recent heavy rains. Donning the life jacket he had brought aboard, he slipped into the cool water and swam for the nearby shore.

Chapter Forty-eight

THE RIVER

"It's not the kind of water cruise I envisioned," Nadia jested to her fellow prisoner above the water's roar.

"But look at the stars," Tanya yelled back. "Lovely night to go boating."

"You don't sound concerned," Nadia remonstrated.

Tanya's response was delayed. "I'm a terrible liar. I'm scared shitless."

"Hey," Nadia said in a hopeful tone, "we don't give up. Not to the end. We still have Del."

Tanya sniffed. "The last time I saw him he was about to join us."

"Something happened to him," Nadia said weakly.

"I noticed," Tanya said. "I'm soaked, and it's cold."

"Say a prayer," Nadia urged.

"It's been a while," Tanya replied. "But it's sure worth a try."

AIRBORNE

"We have to find them fast," the helo pilot said, glancing at Cynthia who was becoming reacquainted with the Black Hawk's controls.

"Not much different," she said. "A few more gauges."

"Want to take over for a bit to get the feel?" the pilot asked.

Cynthia nodded assent and temporarily assumed control before signaling for his seasoned handling. "Thanks, Sam. I feel more confident now."

"You seemed right at home. I feel more confident now too," he said with a grin.

In the cabin of the aircraft, Ryan was helping an HRT operator sweep the searchlight across the river in search of the raft. The eyes of Cynthia and the other operators were busily scanning the terrain.

"Look out for power lines," the pilot told Cynthia. "Has to be at least one around."

It was a full five-minute tension-filled period before Ryan called out, "There they are!" The pilot brought the helo around and began to orbit over the small craft that was bouncing around on the churning water below.

"There's rocks all around," the pilot remarked. "They could be thrown against any one of the big ones."

"Could be the unusually high water level of the flood water coming downstream that's keeping them above most of them," Ryan speculated. "Lots of rain lately."

"They see us!" Cynthia exclaimed. "One of them is kicking her leg like a Radio City Music Hall Rockette."

"Line it up, Sam," Ryan told the pilot as he donned a harness and grabbed a life jacket. "I'm going down."

"We usually do that," an HRT operator said.

"Humor me," Ryan replied. "It's been a while, but I've done plenty. You guys handle the winch."

"Take these," Del said, handing Ryan a pair of wire cutters from Tanya's satchel. "They might come in handy."

Ryan felt the trench knife strapped to his leg. "Can't hurt," he said pocketing the tool.

Minutes later the helicopter was hovering a hundred feet above the raft, and Ryan was descending on the moving target at the end of a sturdy steel cable. A light northerly wind had the helo flying sideways as Ryan swayed a few feet above the raft. Signaling for a few more feet of cable, he dropped to the undulating raft and grabbed a naked leg.

"I've never been happier to have a guy feel my leg," Tanya said. "Welcome, big boy."

"We're not home yet," Ryan replied, examining the shackles, and speaking to Nadia. "I can take one at a time, lady."

"Take her," Nadia said. "She's younger."

"But not as pretty," Ryan said. "Don't go away. I'll be back."

"I'll be here," Nadia said with a wry smile.

"Glad Del gave me the wire cutters," Ryan shouted to be heard above the roar of the helo's engines as he worked on the plastic cuffs linking Tanya to the raft.

"He's a thinker," she said as Ryan severed the connection.

"I thought you said stinker," Nadia joked with feigned levity.

"Here's a life jacket with a strobe light," Ryan said to Nadia, unhooking the orange colored vest from his gear. "It'll help us keep you in sight. I'm also going to cut your cuff connection to the raft, just in case you have to ditch before I get back." After cutting the plastic ties, he helped her into the life vest. "Meanwhile," he said, "hang on tight to the metal ring."

"I'm glad I know how to swim," she said, watching Ryan wrap the harness around Tanya.

With a hand signal to the crew chief, the pair began their ascent, Tanya desperately squeezing her rescuer. After swinging on the end of the cable for what seemed forever to Tanya, they reached the open helo door and were hauled in by eager helping hands.

Tanya's only garment, her water soaked silk robe, was almost transparent as she lay stretched out on the aircraft's metal floor, gulping air.

"Nice catch," one HRT operator commented to a partner, helping Tanya into a warming space blanket before returning to his other duties.

"You're bleeding!" Del exclaimed as Ryan began to rearrange the harness for his return effort.

"Damn," Ryan said, seeing blood flowing from a shoulder wound. "Must have cut it coming through the door."

"Medic!" Del called out, and seconds later an EMT trained operator was administrating to Ryan.

"We still need to get Nadia," Del shouted, grabbing the harness. Before anyone could intervene, Del was strapping himself into the hoist equipment.

"What are you doing?" Ryan asked with surprise.

"Going to get Nadia," Del declared, bundling up.

"But you're not trained," Ryan protested.

"Did it before," Del said, recalling the time he fast-roped from an HRT helicopter onto the deck of a yacht sailing off Atlantic City in the SHARKS case. "Let's go," he yelled to the crew chief operating the winch, as he disappeared over the side of the aircraft.

What have I done? Del asked himself moments later as he dangled in midair some one hundred feet above the water. Then, suddenly, he felt a sudden upward jerk, and he was no longer a hundred from earth, but more like two hundred. Holy Moly, he thought, commencing to mentally recite prayers of petition.

* * *

"Glad you spotted the power line," the pilot commended Cynthia after the helo descended to its original altitude. "We could have had a really bad day."

"To say nothing about the guy dangling below us. You reacted admirably, Sam. I'm impressed."

"We do a lot of training, Cynthia. Now, have you picked up sight of the raft?"

"Yes, thanks to the strobe light. It's moving fast. And, it's getting awfully close to the Great Falls rocks."

"In addition to the training, we also do a lot of praying," the pilot murmured, maneuvering his aircraft into position above the bobbing raft.

Skimming through the atmosphere felt exhilarating to Del, as did the sight of Nadia, illuminated by the helo's spotlights, waving at him from the raft that was now just a few feet away.

The northerly wind had increased, forcing the pilot to crab his aircraft sideways to permit a drop to the raft's deck. Del was almost ready to drop when a wind gust forced him out of range. He could see the disappointment on Nadia's face as he swung away.

After a hand signal to the crew chief operating the hoist for a little more cable, Del was better positioned and the second approach was more successful, with Del landing with a thud on the edge of the raft. Nadia rushed to his arms, and he hastily fastened the harness gear around them both.

"I see big rocks right ahead," Nadia yelled over the roar of the rapids, just as Del signaled lift and their feet left the raft's surface. Spinning in space, their eyes watched in astonishment as the raft tumbled over the edge of the falls.

Clinging together tenaciously, their heart beats slowly receded as they were slowly reeled in.

"Kamsahabnida, sahumnim!" Nadia said. "It's a Tae Kwon Do phrase in Korean, meaning thank you, sir."

And thank you, Lord, was Del's silent prayer.

Lifted over the skids four minutes later, they were quickly back in the Black Hawk's cabin, encased in space blankets and voicing profuse thanks.

Ryan looked at Del and nodded. "Dutton said you were different."

Del smiled agreement and turned to the rescued women. "Bet they don't have as much fun in Russia."

* * *

Within minutes they were back at Algonkian Park, the helo settling down near the Mobile Command Center where the pilot shut down his engines.

Cheers sounded as the blanket-clad survivors emerged from the HRT helo.

Ryan helped Tanya embark, his large white bandage shining in the glow of the parking lot lights. "Let me know if you ever need a workout," she said. "You squeeze nicely."

"He's taken," Cynthia emphasized as she followed closely behind.

"I'd be honored to fly with you any time," the pilot said, shaking Cynthia's hand warmly.

"Likewise, Sam. You're an ace in my book. Anyone who can drop a guy at night on a moving target like you did is a true Top Gun."

Nadia came through the door next, guided by Del who grasped her arm firmly.

The remainder of the crew followed, also loudly applauded by the crowd.

Dutton asked Ryan what had happened to him, and listened as he explained. "You couldn't stay away from the action, could you?" he said with admiration when Ryan finished. "Hope the HRT feathers weren't ruffled when you intervened. They're a proud bunch, rightly so."

"I sort of pulled rank," Ryan said. "May have overstepped."

"They'll get over it. So, who went down for the second woman?"

"Del."

"Del!"

"Yeah, couldn't stop him. He was garbed and out the door before anyone could object. Claimed he had experience."

"Good Lord! And he brought her back?"

"Yep. You told me he was something else. He sure is."

Dutton shook his head. "Wonder how we can write this up for headquarters and get commendations and not suspensions?"

"Just stress the results, boss. Bad guys caught, victims rescued, spy ring broken, two Russian defectors secured, plus one asylum seeker. You're a good writer."

Dutton released a happy grin. "You're right, I need to think positive and count our blessings. Like you, my top Supervisor. Well done, Kevin."

""Thanks, boss. It's been fun."

"Now, where's Nadia? I have the good news she's been seeking."

Ryan pointed to a bench where Nadia was huddled with Curt Oswald, sipping from a cup of hot coffee.

Dutton approached her. "Welcome back to the free world. I have news for you."

Nadia's eyes brightened in anticipation.

"Your grandparents are out. They're currently en route to Canada, and will be in Washington by tomorrow."

"Thank God," Nadia screamed with delight and jumped up to hug Dutton. "You kept your word."

"We believe in promises made, promises kept," Dutton responded. "We had an agreement to honor."

"How did it go down?" Oswald asked as Nadia danced around joyfully.

"Our Agency friends managed to slip them into a tour group headed for Amsterdam, then got them immediately on a flight to Ottawa. Nicely done. They'll be in the U.S. within 24 hours."

In her animated spirit, Nadia spotted Del and Anna who were quietly relaxing on another bench and rushed over to convey the good news. She embraced Del enthusiastically, whispering in his ear, "Don't forget your bosom buddy."

"Everyone needs a good night's rest," Dutton addressed the group. "Tomorrow's a holiday with pay for all of you. We'll take care of the paper work the following day."

A round of applause erupted.

"I'll be in the office in the afternoon," he added, "after I take Rambo to the vet for x-rays."

"How's he doing?" Ryan asked.

"Moving slowly, but hopefully not too badly hurt by that bastard."

"Who is where now?" Ryan asked.

"Federal lockup at the Loudoun County Jail, along with his two goons. Agents arrested Viktor Markov in his cab in Arlington."

"And Alexei?"

Dutton frowned. "Our missing link. There's an all-out search for him. Our case isn't closed."

"I'll see you in the office tomorrow afternoon, boss."

As the Mobile Command van lumbered away, and the others departed in various combinations, Del and Anna embraced in the rear seat of Moretti and Summer's Bureau sedan being driven to the Westin Hotel in Tysons Corner.

"I'm anxious to hear all about your experiences with those two Russian beauties," Anna cooed.

Del feigned sleep.

Epilogue

A month later, Dutton invited all of what he called his All Stars to a backyard cookout at his residence. "Revisit the scene of the crime," was the wording on the invitations his wife, Lydia, designed.

The Indian Summer weather was delightfully warm as the group gathered in his spacious yard. Beverages, hard and soft, were handily placed in coolers around the property. A fully stocked bar stood ready on the patio, next to a row of grills that promised a variety of tasty food. Hovering over the culinary promises was a beaming woman of sturdy build and pleasant disposition. "I am Olga," she informed everyone, "and I happy to be here. Have some of my goulash," she added, pointing at a handle-less pot on a warming burner.

Rambo roamed around with ease, a red, white, and blue bandana tied around his neck.

The HRT team arrived together in a Bureau SUV, prepared for a 4-hour response requirement that limited their beverage consumption. "There's always tomorrow," one operator said with a reassuring wink. Sam Carr, the helo pilot needled his co-pilot, Jeff Williams, whose right arm remained in a protective cast. "My emergency co-pilot is certainly prettier than you."

Williams was quick to retort, "Yeah, but would she take a bullet for you, and put up with your jerky flying?"

"Let's have a beer," Carr suggested.

Nadia arrived with an attentive Curt Oswald, their verbal interchanges seemingly a very comfortable dialogue. She was dressed casually in a leisure suit that failed to conceal her provocative figure.

Tanya was escorted by Cynthia and Ryan, sharing spirited and jocular conversation. She was dressed modestly in tennis shorts and loose blouse, with a leather necklace dangling sterling silver medallions that looked like miniature hatchets.

Del and Anna were warmly welcomed, seemingly fully recovered from their respective challenges. He was clean shaven, hair newly trimmed. She looked intriguingly exotic in a cotton pantsuit with gold oriental trim.

The rest of the guests milled about, exchanging recollections of their participation in "the case."

Assistant Director Wayne Jackson, and his wife, Mona, arrived shortly before Dutton invited everyone to gather around.

"First," Dutton said, "I want to update you on the latest business, our search for Alexei Nikolay."

"Yeah," someone asked, "what happened to him?"

Dutton smiled. "Justice, perhaps. You know he bailed out at the tip of parkland abutting the Potomac. Well, there have been a number of sightings of bears there, scaring the hell out of park visitors."

With the full attention of his audience, Dutton went on. "So, the park service set out a few bear traps, humane of course, and Alexei got caught in one."

Several claps were heard before Dutton continued. "He was there all night, and half the next day until a camper heard his cries. Meanwhile, a number of insects had a feast. He's now under guard at the Loudoun County Hospital, where he was arraigned and ordered held for trial. He can walk with assistance, but will always have a limp."

"What a pity," a female voice with a Russian accent said in a sarcastic tone.

"There is some good news to report," Ryan interjected: "Nadia's grandparents are now in the United States." Hearty applause erupted.

Dutton resumed speaking. "I'd also like to introduce a prospective new citizen," he said, gesturing to the cook. "Olga Servadova was a great help to our prisoners."

The woman beamed graciously and rubbed her hands on her apron. "But he has to return the pot handle he stole," she said, pointing to Del. "No crime allowed in America!"

"I'm guilty," Del declared amidst the laughter. "I'll buy you a new pot."

Dutton then proceeded to report that Congressmen Walters and Palmer, and Congresswoman Rasmussen, were all indicted on various charges and released on bail awaiting trial. "Widespread negative publicity in their home states make it highly unlikely that any of them could be re-elected," he concluded.

"And Anna," he said with a smile, "reports that calls to her from Walters are returned by a friend who advises him that she has left town with her insurance salesman."

Assistant Director Jackson then assumed the podium, which resembled the top of a Heineken half-keg. "The Director sends his congratulations to all of you for your outstanding work," he began. He proceeded to enumerate the accomplishments of the awardees, and presented checks representing financial incentive awards. "Letters of commendation are also on the way for the rest of you," he concluded.

During the ceremony, Rambo wandered between Del and Dutton, hovering close to Del when he softly whistled *Yankee Doodle Dandy*. With a grin, Dutton responded in kind, causing the confused dog to roam back and forth between the men.

As dusk approached, a church bell was heard ringing in the distance, backed by the hum of planes on a landing approach path. Faces turned to the sounds, smiles emerging. "Old investigative techniques still work," Dutton remarked to Ryan.

"When do we eat?" Del yelled, generating loud laughter.

"Steaks, shrimp, and rockfish on the grills, side dishes on the platters," Dutton announced. "Help yourselves, after we give thanks," he said, gesturing to Oswald, the former seminarian. "Guess you're the in-house chaplain, Curt."

Following the brief ecumenical blessing, Olga yelled in her heavy accent, "Don't forget my goulash. Good for you."

"You should have heard the screams from the Russian Embassy when we advised them of the arrests," Jackson said to Dutton as they worked on their meals.

"I can imagine. What was our response?"

Jackson chuckled after devouring a piece of spiced shrimp. "Officially, we simply told them their employees were charged with serious U.S. crimes. Unofficially, our message was 'screw you.' The relationship is somewhat strained these days, you might say."

Casual conversation was flourishing among the guests when Olga gained everyone's attention by banging a serving spoon on her goulash pot. "Nadia have something to say."

Striding forward, Nadia launched a bright smile. "I am happy to announce that Tanya and I are opening a Tae Kwon Do studio in Fairfax, near the Russian Orthodox church that Tanya recently joined. In addition to a good workout, you'll have access to good food. Olga will operate a small snack shop on the premises. It's our American dream." A round of congratulatory applause followed.

When sensor-operated patio lights began to flicker on, Dutton again thanked the attendees for their part in the operations and suggested a parting song.

"*God Bless America*," Nadia suggested, leading the group in a spirited rendition before the group began to disperse.

Special Agent Moretti approached Tanya to say he might be interested in visiting her new studio. "Being single, I have a little spare time," he said, initiating a sparkle in Tanya's blue eyes, and a business card with her address and phone number.

Nadia cornered Del and Anna to inform them that she and her grandparents were moving into a two-bedroom apartment in the same building.

"No ceiling mirrors," she added with a wink to Del that wasn't missed by Anna.

Assistant Director Jackson spent a few private minutes with Dutton before departing. "You live well, Andy, and you've earned it. I wish we had more dedicated administrators like you in the hierarchy."

"People like you keep us going," Dutton replied. "We've both come a long way from new agent's training, and you're a fine example of exceptional performance."

"We sound like a mutual admiration society," Jackson chuckled. "But, seriously, you'd have made a great Director."

"Thanks, Wayne, and I say with utmost sincerity, so would you."

"One day perhaps," the black administrator replied wistfully. "It seems that some retire too early. It will be the Bureau's loss when you reach mandatory retirement in a few years. Meanwhile, I imagine you are sometimes tempted to accept that employment offer from Lockheed-Martin resting in your desk drawer."

"Not many secrets are there?" Dutton replied. "But, I have no early plans to leave."

"That's encouraging, Andy. I'd hate to have you gone when we go to trial on these cases."

Dutton nodded. "Yeah, the final curtain hasn't yet fallen. I'll be around for a while."

Ryan walked up as Jackson and his wife were departing, thanking Dutton for the special party. "You've really given me an education, boss."

"You've been a great student, Kevin. Sorry you got wounded."

"A scratch, Andy. The SEALS would treat it like a hangnail."

"I see you have good nursing care," Dutton said with a grin.

Ryan smiled back. "Cynthia has displayed many talents. We also discovered a common interest in water para-gliding. We'll be out this coming weekend on a friend's boat near Annapolis."

"Excellent choice," Dutton said with an approving clasp of Ryan's good shoulder as Del and Anna approached.

"We'll be leaving, sir," Del said, "and I want to thank you for all you've done for Anna and me."

"It's the other way around, young man," Dutton replied with emphasis. "You and Anna made the cases. You both performed superbly."

"Just doing our jobs, Mr. Dutton. We also want to say goodbye. We're heading back to San Francisco tomorrow afternoon."

Dutton hugged Anna, and shook Del's hand warmly. "We haven't forgotten about the laundered money," he said to Anna. "It still might end up in your bank account after all the legal proceedings." He turned to Del. "You have a priceless gem here, young man, and maybe a very rich one at that. I suggest you treat her well."

Del nodded. "I know what genuine wealth is, sir. We look forward to seeing you again."

Dutton and Ryan waved goodbye to the departing couple. "You told me about your apprehensions about Del, and I thought you were exaggerating," Ryan said. "You've made a believer out of me."

Dutton laughed. "Yeah, seeing is believing, isn't it? But we survived!"

"For the time being, Andy."

"What do you mean?"

"They'll both have to return to testify, of course."

Dutton slapped his forehead. "Good Lord! That slipped my mind."

"Understandable, boss, with all that's been going on. Happens to us all."

Driving into the darkening night, Anna snuggled against Del's shoulder. "It's been quite an adventure, my love, and I feel so blessed that we are both still alive."

"We're both blessed and lucky, Anna."

"Yes," she sighed. "I was so worried when I heard that you were confined in that cold cellar, and wondered how you kept warm. Well, we'll have our whole cross-country trip tomorrow to talk about it."

Del gulped.

BONUS FEATURE

Follow other adventures of Del Dickerson in FLYING HIGH: FBI vs. The Mob.

FLYING HIGH: FBI vs. The Mob

Chapter One

The Mountains

God, I need a man, Kerry Vita muttered, striding from the small rustic cabin into crisp mountain air. Low forties, she guessed, watching her breath vaporize. She raised the zipper of the dark-blue jacket that hugged her curvaceous figure, and pulled the jacket hood over cropped raven hair. Shouldering a white canvas bag, holding easel, palette, paints, and canvasses, she hurried down the narrow path leading to her favorite painting site. The twenty-five-year-old ivory-complexioned woman glanced up at the milky contrails of a high-flying jet darting through random cumulus clouds. Up, up, and away, she thought, sort of like me.

With a flick of her right thumb, the pristine stillness was shattered by the intrusion of a country-western ballad flowing from the compact transistor radio she'd found in a cabin drawer. One station, girl. Get used to it. A slight smile parted her generous lips as she thought of the vibrant music she was accustomed to, and the rapt audiences roaring approval. *There's a Broken Heart for Every Light on Broadway* came to mind, and a shadow of sadness clouded her classic features as she thought of Jeff. Now, there was a man! What a damned waste! A grimace of determination firmed her delicate jaw. I owe you Nicky, you bastard, and I won't forget.

The golden rays of the morning sun sliced through towering pine trees and highlighted the view of the snow-clad mountain peaks miles away.

Thoughts of New York, Jeff, and the past, even Nicky the bastard, evaporated as she propelled her energies into a life-long avocation. Thanks, Mom, for the talent, and rest in the peace you never enjoyed on earth.

The warmth generated by her energetic preparations so steadied her hands that her first brush strokes were firm and fluid despite the chilled atmosphere. The long-range vista forming on her canvas held her full attention for over an hour, until the engine drone of a small airplane slowly orbiting above the massive valley penetrated her consciousness. She looked up at the intruder with annoyance. *Can't a girl even enjoy some peace and quiet out here?*

She tried to refocus on her painting, but kept shifting attention to the small plane that now bounced around from the unpredictable updrafts characterizing the valley. Concentration broken, she guessed it was time for a smoke. *Except you gave that up, too,* she reminded herself. She collapsed into the old deck chair she had installed in the mountainside clearing and resumed her study of the bobbing aircraft that had steadily gained altitude. Momentarily closing her eyes, she thought of the circumstances that brought her to this place. She also listened to the echo of the plane's laboring engines, and pondered the nature of the people aboard. *I wonder what your stories are.*

The Sky

"Is this what you guys do on a day off?" shouted the jumpmaster to the parachute-clad young man perched near the open door of the King Air.

"Beats fishing," FBI agent Del Dickerson shouted back with a grin, adjusting the straps of his multi-colored chute. "Of course, my fiancée thinks I'm crazy, and my bosses aren't too keen on the risks, but if it's good enough for President Bush 41, I guess I'm in good company."

Jesse, the crewman, shook his head. "His wife isn't too happy about it, I understand."

Del nodded. "But his survival skills are legendary. I hope I'm as lucky."

"The winds have really picked up," Jesse cautioned, "and Magic Valley is notorious for surprises. Sure you don't want to put this off a day?"

"It's my last day here. Then, I'm back to the office. Today is now or never."

"Never isn't a bad option sometimes," Jesse commented.

The muscular, sandy-haired agent looked reflective, gazing at the wiry skydiving instructor and then at the broad valley below. "I appreciate your concern, but I've established a rather bizarre reputation for doing goofy things. Weird incidents seem to happen to me, and people around me." Mental images flashed through his mind, like the time he stumbled into a Knoxville chop-shop and broke up an interstate auto theft ring. And the time he was kidnapped with a potential father-in-law and forced in the man's presence into a sexual act with their captor's comely girlfriend in an effort to effect their escape. He smiled at another recollection of the time he became an instant hero when he shot a pit bull attacking the Mississippi governor's granddaughter outside the state mansion. He grinned. "No, I'm ready to go, unless you insist to the contrary."

Jesse shook his head. "It's marginal, but I'd probably do it."

Del raised his right thumb. "That's good enough for me. Let's go." He moved against the strong wind pressure rushing through the open cabin door, while the jumpmaster radioed the impending jump to the pilot.

"We'll wait till we level off at 10,000 feet. Remember the location of the handle of your emergency chute, and keep aiming for the designated landing zone. And, good luck. I'll see you back at the airport."

Del nodded understanding, sensed the plane leveling, saw the green light flash, felt the firm thump on his shoulder, and leaped forward into space.

The City

Nicky "The Nose" Vincente screamed obscenities at the two swarthy thugs cowering before him in the cramped, smoke-saturated office of Brooklyn's Bossa Ristorante Italiano. "What the fuck good are you two pricks if you can't find one scrawny broad?"

Louis Milano, known as "Loose Louie," due to chronically defective bowel controls, made the mistake of correcting his employer as he envisioned the exciting contours of the missing woman. "She never looked scrawny to me, boss."

Vincente glared. "You fuckin moron, all you think about is pussy. If I say she's scrawny, she's scrawny."

Loose Louie gulped. "You're right, boss, scrawny." He was relieved to hear his partner divert attention.

"We looked everywhere, Nicky, all the places she used to hang at. She just disappeared without a trace."

The ambitious, fortyish member of the embattled Gambino crime family shifted attention to Salvatore Rinalti, also known as "Sulfur Sal" for his expertise in disposing of bodies of adversaries in drums of sulfuric acid. He adjusted his black-rimmed glasses on his prominent nose and snorted disbelief. "No one just disappears without a trace, unless, of course, you practiced your specialty." His scowl was momentarily replaced by a glimmer of grudging admiration. "What are you doing to find her?"

"We got all the boys checking their sources," Loose Louie assured. "It's only a matter of time."

"It's been almost a month already. I'm losing patience." He glared at the two hirelings who watched the rapid movement of their leader's eyebrows that twitched spasmodically when he was agitated. "If you'd completed the job when you whacked her old man and the boyfriend, we wouldn't be in this fuckin mess now."

"She must have been tipped," Sulfur Sal parried. "Slipped out a back window or something."

"With the fuckin book," Vincente reminded.

His lieutenants looked uncomfortably at the floor, then at each other.

Vincente continued fulminating. "Now I gotta go to another fuckin meeting and explain that my two hot-shot soldiers can't find one scrawny broad."

"Right, boss, a scrawny broad," Loose Louie quickly agreed, again mentally undressing the traffic-stopping figure of the missing woman.

Vincente took off his glasses and placed them atop a case of imported extra-virgin olive oil stacked next to his desk. He wearily rubbed his blood-shot brown eyes that had immediately crossed when the glasses were removed. "You guys are living on borrowed time," he hissed. "I don't know how long I can hold off the boys from replacing you."

The message was deathly clear. Sulfur Sal blanched and croaked, "They won't have to do that, boss. We'll find her."

Loose Louie shuffled his feet nervously. "I gotta go to the can."

Kudos for FLYING HIGH

"Jim Healy uses his years of service with the FBI to put together an accurate portrayal of how this elite organization functions. FLYING HIGH has it all: intrigue, romance, thrills and an exhilarating climax. Along the way, the reader can see how the FBI utilizes all legal methods available to solve crimes and thwart criminal elements such as the Mafioso." —**John Wagner**, FBI Special Agent in Charge, Retired.

Retired FBI agent Jim Healy has successfully transformed his many years of chasing the mob into a delightful novel that covers stories of love, comedy, and intrigue, based on actual events he experienced during his long career. A must read that will keep you turning pages to the end. —**Edgar E. DeLong**, LCDR USN (Ret), author of *NAVY MUSTANG*.

Jim Healy's new novel FLYING HIGH (pun intended I'm sure), doesn't wait for the reader to catch up to the story; rather, it plunges him or her into the crisp writing of this page-turning narrative, punctuated by Healy's ear for dialogue and language, and old fashioned and suspenseful story telling ability. The reader, in the midst of the story, just hangs on; and it is a fun and pleasant ride laced with humor and at times, dark irony. While this book is not about the FBI per se, many characters in it, from those in the Mob to Special Agents, are informed by Healy's substantial experience as an FBI agent and executive. —**I.B. Wells**, Retired FBI Special Agent in Charge, author of *Women of Summer*.

Other Special Agent Del Dickerson novels
Available from Amazon.com in paperback, and Kindle E-Book

FLYING HIGH:FBI vs. THE MOB

Adventurous FBI agent Del Dickerson accidentally parachutes into a grove of trees in California and is rescued by lovely Greenwich Village band singer Kerry Vita, hiding out from the New York mob in her aunt's isolated mountain cabin with damning gang payoff records. Tending Del's broken leg, she falls in love.

Bumbling Mafia hit men, Loose Louie Milano, and Sulfur Sal Rinalti, race west from New York to recover the records and kill Kerry. FBI agents, and Del's Amerasian fiancée, Anna Chen, frantically search for him, and a female agent is taken captive in a bizarre nudist camp. Rescuers and assassins converge simultaneously, igniting chaotic action. A fortuitous discovery by Del saves the day, and he, Kerry, and Anna survive to ponder a triangular romantic future.

Spiced with conflict, intrigue, romance and humor, FLYING HIGH takes you inside the real-life world of the FBI.

LUCKY DAZE: FBI vs. THE MOB-REMATCH

Unconventional FBI Agent Del Dickerson swerves from one hair-raising adventure to another as he again pursues escaped mob hit men Loose Louie Milano and Sulfur Sal Rinalti, with action exploding in San Francisco, Salt Lake City, Sacramento, Reno, and the Sierra Nevada mountains.

Major characters from FLYING HIGH reappear in this fast-moving novel which introduces new personalities, including attractive blonde agent Janice Wilson, another complication in Del's romantic minefield. The serious side of FBI work is illustrated by a deadly shoot-out in San Francisco with a psychotic killer, driving the surviving Janice into Del's comforting arms.

Enjoy an inside look at the lives and loves of memorable FBI investigators, while you laugh at the bumbling antics of Loose Louie and Sulfur Sal, and learn how the wild search, and Del's ingenuity, lead to a fiery conclusion.

FBI Code Name: SHARKS, Fighting Washington Corruption

Young, impetuous Special Agent Del Dickerson stumbles into a multi-million dollar commodities conspiracy between unscrupulous lobbyists and dishonest Washington legislators. He becomes romantically involved with Amerasian beauty Anna Chen, consort of a powerful corrupt Senator guiding the fraud. New agent Lola Stanley, a former Radio City Music Hall Rockette, goes undercover as an Atlantic City chorus girl to penetrate the plot. Fast-moving action, loaded with humor and intrigue, explodes in Norfolk, Washington, and Atlantic City, culminating in a thrilling climax when FBI Hostage Rescue Team operators drop from helicopters onto a luxury yacht at sea.

FBI Code Name: CULTURED PEARL, Smuggled Terror

Amerasian beauty Anna Chen holds the key to deciphering the diary of a disgraced United States Senator involved in international smuggling of precious gems and nuclear devices. Targeted for assassination by White House and Justice Department conspirators, Anna is defended by quixotic FBI Special Agent Del Dickerson, noted for inexplicable good luck until he is shot. Action-packed adventures explode from Virginia and Washington, D.C., to the Canadian border. Danger, adventure, intrigue, and romance enrich this fast-paced story of greed, betrayal, and redemption. CULTURED PEARL has it all!

FBI Code Name: DEADLY DECEPTION, Murder in Monterey

Fictional Special Agent Del Dickerson, known for unorthodox behavior and phenomenal luck, studying Korean at the Foreign Language Institute in Monterey, California, finds himself in the middle of a Chinese-Communist plot to assassinate his professor.

A Taiwanese Army officer classmate is the prime suspect, possibly aided by Del's beautiful Amerasian fiancée. Complicating his turbulent life is the unexpected arrival of a former lover with matrimonial intentions. A murder, poisoning, aircraft hijacking, and kidnapping generate fast-moving action between Monterey and San Francisco, culminating in a dramatic Nob Hill raid by an FBI SWAT team, where dels' ingenuity thwarts the murderous intentions of a psychotic assassin known as "Scorpion."

ABOUT THE AUTHOR

The wide-eyed Detroit youngster avidly following the exploits of J. Edgar Hoover's G-Men battling Dillinger-era gangsters never imagined that he would one day be on the headquarters' staff of the legendary FBI Director. Jim Healy realized that dream, joining Hoover's relentless fight against crime and communism.

Following two years in the U.S. Navy during World War II, the author earned a Journalism degree at Michigan State University and applied for FBI employment. Underage for the Agent's position, he began as Night Clerk in the Detroit office while attending the University of Detroit Law School. Three years later, he graduated from the FBI Academy as a Special Agent and headed west.

In Seattle and Tacoma, Washington, he investigated a variety of crimes before being transferred to San Francisco where he tracked communist spies throughout northern California.

Upon the collapse of the Communist Party underground apparatus, he was transferred to FBI Headquarters where he subsequently directed the famed Ten Most Wanted Fugitives Program for thirteen years. Murderers, kidnappers, and bank robbers were his favorite fugitives to place on the "Top Ten" list. A believer in gender equality, he takes credit for adding the first woman to the list.

Returning to field investigations, he led the search for the first escapees from the "escape-proof" Federal Penitentiary at Marion, Illinois, built as a replacement for Alcatraz. After other challenging field assignments, he retired in Norfolk, Virginia, as Special Agent in Charge. He then spent ten years as Vice President of an international security firm in Washington, D.C., before settling in Virginia Beach and becoming active in civic, fraternal, community, church, and writing pursuits.

The proud father of six, he writes from his comfortable retreat on the Chesapeake Bay.

www.ingramcontent.com/pod-product-compliance
Lightning Source LLC
LaVergne TN
LVHW051111080426
835510LV00018B/1999